Stay Awhile

Also by Kara Eidson

A Time to Grow: Lenten Lessons from the Garden to the Table

Stay Awhile

Advent Lessons in Divine Hospitality

KARA EIDSON

WESTMINSTER
JOHN KNOX PRESS
LOUISVILLE · KENTUCKY

First edition
Published by Westminster John Knox Press
Louisville, Kentucky

23 24 25 26 27 28 29 30 31 32—10 9 8 7 6 5 4 3 2 1

Book design by Drew Stevens
Chapter opening image from Vecteezy.com
Cover design by Allison Taylor

Library of Congress Cataloging-in-Publication Data is on file
at the Library of Congress, Washington, DC.

ISBN-13: 978-0-664-26842-8

Most Westminster John Knox Press books are available at special quantity discounts when purchased in bulk by corporations, organizations, and special–interest groups. For more information, please e–mail SpecialSales@wjkbooks.com.

To my parents, Ken and Wanda Eidson:

Thank you for all the ways you have both taught me to create spaces in which people know they are loved and then want to stay awhile.

Contents

Introduction

I am long on staying, I am slow to leave,
especially when it comes to you, my friend.
You have taught me to slow down and to prop up my feet,
it's the fine art of being who I am.

Sara Groves, "Every Minute"

*I*n the Midwest, there is a common invitation when you come to visit and someone wants you to stick around: "Why don't you pull up a chair and stay awhile?" In a fast-food, packed-schedule, stay-busy culture, the notion of staying awhile has grown a little bit foreign. But sometimes, slowing down and staying awhile is exactly what we need. It is the only way to form deep relationships with others; it is the only way to form a deep relationship with God.

Nothing worthwhile comes quickly or easily. Good things take work to develop, time to mature, and energy to grow. Of the many lessons I took away from my experiences of isolation during the COVID-19 pandemic, there is one I hope to carry throughout my life: few endeavors are more precious than the time we spend with other people—and there is no substitute for quality time.

When guests are scheduled to arrive in our homes, very few of us simply throw open the doors and announce, "We're ready!" The normal state of my home and kitchen are what my father-in-law lovingly refers to as "lived-in," so my husband and I will spend time preparing prior to the arrival of beloved guests. In the same way, Christians must also spend time preparing our hearts, minds, and souls for the coming Christ. We are called to active anticipation and to do the sacred work of Advent while we wait.

In this Advent study, we will explore how we provide hospitality for guests in our homes, how that extends into our spiritual lives, and how we can apply these lessons to the season of Advent. While understandings of hospitality may vary with setting and culture, as I contemplated the goal of hospitality, I kept coming back to the idea of making another person feel at home. Not always to the home of actual childhood—some people did not find the warm embrace they ought to have there—but what home ought to be: a place where we can be authentically and completely ourselves and where we always know that we will be safe and loved. A place where we can heal and rest from the weariness of a world that has the tendency to wear and weigh us down, despite its infinite amount of beauty. I don't spend a lot of time considering the specifics of heaven, but I suspect arriving there is similar to the moment of hearing those long-awaited words, "Welcome home." The traveler, the student, the wanderer, the soldier, the castaway, the estranged, the unloved, the abused, the broken: we have all longed for those beloved words.

Our brains are hardwired to this setting of home in ways so deeply embedded in us that we cannot consciously adjust them. Sleep studies have shown that half of the brain doesn't enter REM sleep the first night or two that we sleep in a new place. From an evolutionary standpoint, when we sleep in a new place, half of our brain is staying alert, wondering, "Is there a bear in this new cave with me? Will a lion try to eat me during the night?" Despite knowing logically that we are safe and sound in a hotel room, or perfectly safe in a friend's or family member's home, biologically our brains are still wired to be on alert when we sleep in new environments.[1] Even the sleeping brain can tell when we are at home.

So, the ultimate goal of hospitality is to help people feel as if they are "at home" in this archetypal sense, to invite and welcome them into a space that is not their own dwelling and provide an encounter in which they feel safe and loved.

In an academic paper published in 1943, psychologist Abraham Maslow presented a theory that came to be known as Maslow's hierarchy of needs. The theory proposes that only when certain needs are met can human beings then seek the fulfillment of their needs on the next level. For example, he proposed that humans will not seek out fulfillment of needs such as belonging and love when our physiological needs (for water, food, shelter, etc.) are unmet. While the order, cultural implications, and divisions of Maslow's originally proposed hierarchy have been topics of heated debate in academia for decades, there is still truth to be found in the basic premise; we know instinctively that a starving person will be more concerned with bread than with spiritual enlightenment. Similarly, I believe that experiencing God's kin-dom here on earth requires spaces in which we first feel safe and loved.

Throughout this book, I have chosen to use the word "kin-dom" rather than "kingdom." Ada María Isasi-Díaz, the mother of *mujerista* theology, embraced the term "kin-dom" and brought it into modern theological circles through her work. Having heard the phrase at a monastic retreat, it became a central part of her theology. The word "kingdom" carries insinuations of monarchy and colonialism and even—when applied in theology—engenders God as distinctly male. The use of "kin-dom" transforms the possibilities for God's reign on earth, and it becomes a place in which humans live as equals, and everyone serves one another. "Kin" implies family—a familiarity—that "kingdom" lacks.

This familial sense that accompanies the use of "kin-dom" addresses the need for belonging that exists within all human beings and is even included in Maslow's original hierarchy. We are most likely to initially encounter the kin-dom of God in spaces where others provide intentional hospitality, offering us spaces of love and safety. When we begin to be participants in kin-dom building, it then becomes our obligation to extend that hospitality to other people so that they might also experience the beauty of God's kin-dom here on earth.

When we participate in moments of excellent hospitality, we catch glimpses into the kin-dom of God. There are thin spaces in this world where heaven and earth brush up against each other. Within these thin spaces, we catch glimpses of God's kin-dom. We catch glimpses of what we mean when we dutifully pray, "Thy kingdom come, thy will be done, on earth as it is in heaven," during the Lord's Prayer. We enter sacred space when we offer and receive hospitality, share in abundance, and stay awhile. The thin spaces between heaven and earth that I have experienced most frequently have not been in church pews or on mountaintops; they have been gatherings around tables with others, surrounded by laughter and love.

This book explores Advent through the lens of hospitality as I understand it, from a personal viewpoint within my own home and context. This is not a treatise on the diversity of cultural understandings of hospitality, although I would love to read that book! I would be remiss not to mention that excellent hospitality may look very different in other cultural contexts. While I briefly touch on hospitality in other cultures in this book, most of the stories contained are about hospitality from the perspective of my own, midwestern U.S. culture.

While many people in the United States view Thanksgiving as the first day of the cultural Christmas season, the drive of capitalism has urged us to begin "the season of buying" earlier with each year that passes. Because of this, it is not uncommon to see Christmas decorations and items adorning the shelves of some stores as early as September. Around Thanksgiving, nearly every store begins playing Christmas music over its speakers, priming us as shoppers to start stocking up for the holiday.

Because American culture loudly declares, "Christmas is here!" by Thanksgiving, many people are taken aback by the lectionary texts on the First Sunday of Advent. People wonder why the church is talking about the end times, and what's with all the gloom and doom? Where are the shepherds and the cute baby in the manger? The passage we read from Luke on the First Sunday of Advent—"Be alert at all times, praying that you may have the strength to escape all these things that will take place"—is hardly synonymous with the radio playing "All I Want for Christmas Is My Two Front Teeth" or "Little Drummer Boy."

Capitalism and pop culture desperately attempt to co-opt one of Christianity's most sacred and holy seasons, but they get the "spirit of the season" all wrong. In fact, they get the season itself wrong! Christmas—the twelve-day liturgical season celebrating Christ's birth—does not begin until December 25. Advent, the weeks leading up to Christmas, is not a season of celebration—it is a season of waiting, anticipation, and preparation.

This is often a source of contention when pastors and church staff members begin worship planning for Advent. Clergy often wade directly into the tension of wanting to honor the true nature of the

Advent season while struggling to maintain the satisfaction of the people in the pews. A lot of people expect to hear Christmas songs in church the Sunday after Thanksgiving, but I have tried to encourage the communities I serve to put Christmas back where it belongs, because Christmas means so much more when the season of Advent is respected and observed. I frequently begin worship during this season with the greeting, "It is a joy to worship with you as we continue this season of waiting," to remind people that Christmas has not yet arrived.

As a child, I remember seeing all the desserts, cookies, and candies spread out across the table for Christmas Day. Usually these were on a different counter or table than the rest of the Christmas feast. I remember always wanting to start at the dessert table—sometimes I still have this urge. (A good friend has settled this dilemma in her family by having pie for breakfast on Christmas morning!) But, inevitably, a responsible adult will step in and say, "You can't start with dessert—you'll ruin your dinner."

Advent is more spiritually complex than not starting with dessert, but the premise is the same. Filling up at the dessert table may seem like a brilliant idea, but it will leave a person feeling slightly sick from all that sugar. Kicking off Christmas when the world tells us it should begin may seem like a fantastic plan, until we realize that we've lost the spiritual meaning of Christmas amid all the ribbons and candy canes.

Not only is Advent a time of waiting to celebrate, it is a time of waiting for the coming of Christ in the past, present, and future. We await the arrival of the Christ child in the manger in the past, we await the coming of Christ in our hearts in the present, and we await the second coming of Christ in the future. My own denomination acknowledges this belief in our Holy Communion service, with the entire congregation reciting in unison, "Christ has died. Christ has risen. Christ will come again." In Charles Dickens's novel *A Christmas Carol,* Ebenezer Scrooge is visited by the ghosts of Christmas past, present, and future. Recalling the three spirits from the novel can be a helpful tool in remembering Advent as a time when we wait for Jesus' arrival in the past, present, and future.

Stay Awhile includes reflection questions at the end of each chapter that can be utilized by small groups or individuals on their personal spiritual journey through Advent. There is a chapter for each Sunday during Advent and for Christmas Eve, and an additional chapter for Christmas and beyond. There are also themed daily devotions for the season. Advent always begins on a Sunday, but because December 25 can fall on any day of the week, Advent can be different lengths from one year to the next. Depending on the year you are using this resource, there might be extra daily devotions. Readers can choose to skip the extra days or use them and consider them bonus material.

The final chapter of this book includes worship resources for pastors and church staff who incorporate the themes from *Stay Awhile* into their worship throughout the season. These resources include sermon starters, responsive prayers, community questions, prompts for children's time, suggestions for worship arts, and an interactive children's program for Christmas Eve. All Scripture references are from the New Revised Standard Version, and the focus Scriptures are mostly drawn from the Revised Common Lectionary for Advent across years A, B, and C.

A companion video series introducing each session is available on Westminster John Knox Press's YouTube channel. These introductory videos are perfect starting points for group study. Find the entire playlist at http://tiny.cc/StayAwhileVideos.

Hospitality starts with an invitation. So, we begin this study with the theme of invitation on the First Sunday of Advent. Just as we anticipate hosting loved ones by planning our shopping lists and playlists, making preparations for their arrival, and finally swinging open the door to begin the party, this study will move through the themes of plan, prepare, and welcome, finally urging those gathered to "stay awhile" and "don't be a stranger." So, brew up something warm to drink, pull up a chair, and stay awhile. The most precious guest the world has ever known is coming, and we are all called to get ready.

First Sunday of Advent

INVITE

Jeremiah 33:14–16; Luke 21:25–36

The days are surely coming, says the LORD, when I will fulfill the promise I made to the house of Israel and the house of Judah. In those days and at that time I will cause a righteous Branch to spring up for David; and he shall execute justice and righteousness in the land. In those days Judah will be saved and Jerusalem will live in safety. And this is the name by which it will be called: "The LORD is our righteousness."

Jeremiah 33:14–16

"There will be signs in the sun, the moon, and the stars, and on the earth distress among nations confused by the roaring of the sea and the waves. People will faint from fear and foreboding of what is coming upon the world, for the powers of the heavens will be shaken. Then they will see 'the Son of Man coming in a cloud' with power and great glory. Now when these things begin to take place, stand up and raise your heads, because your redemption is drawing near."

Then he told them a parable: "Look at the fig tree and all the trees; as soon as they sprout leaves you can see for yourselves and know that summer is already near. So also, when you see these things taking place, you know that the kingdom of God is near. Truly I tell you, this generation will not pass away until all things have taken place. Heaven and earth will pass away, but my words will not pass away.

"Be on guard so that your hearts are not weighed down with dissipation and drunkenness and the worries of this life, and that day catch you unexpectedly, like a trap. For it will come upon all who live on the face of the whole earth. Be alert at all times, praying that you may have the strength to escape all these things that will take place, and to stand before the Son of Man."

Luke 21:25–36

The first year I served as a pastor in a local church, a church member casually invited me to attend the annual gingerbread house party she hosted in her home. When I arrived at her house, I was surprised to find how vastly she had undersold the event in her invitation. The house was full of people, the kitchen and living room were filled with tables and chairs, cheerful Christmas music played in the background, and royal icing covered most visible surfaces. She scheduled the annual party after winter break had begun, so kids were weaving in and out among the adults; some were focused intently on their gingerbread house decorations, some were more interested in eating the candy intended for decorations. There was an entire table just for the candy options, including candy building blocks and chocolates with a candy coating that made them look like colorful rocks from the bottom of a fish tank. The host began introducing me to everyone, including her friends, family, neighbors, and fellow church members. Some people immediately made room for me at one of the tables, and I joined them in decorating my house but also began to join in the cheerful conversation.

I loved the party so much that I decided to replicate the tradition (in minuscule fashion) with my nieces each year during the holiday season—and it has become a beloved family tradition. When my oldest niece approached her middle school years, being overly aware of how many activities she had declared herself "too old for now," I asked her if she still wanted to decorate gingerbread houses at Christmas. She looked at me with all the sass only a preteen girl can muster and said, "Aunt Kara, that's what we do at Christmas. Of *course* we're decorating gingerbread houses!" A single invitation more than fifteen years ago came to shape how my family celebrates the Christmas season.

When we are invited to be ongoing participants in the kin-dom of God, we are not always aware of the magnitude of what we are being invited to join. We have no idea where the invitation might lead us, but we know we will never be alone. God will be with us.

Did I Get Invited?

Do you remember the first time, in childhood or adolescence, when you heard about the social event of the year? A birthday party, a concert, or a trip that had everyone in your social circle excited? It felt as if everyone was talking about it. And then you received the worst news of all: you weren't invited. Do you remember?

I have several memories like this, but the one that sticks out was one New Year's Eve when I was in high school. My group of friends were all going to a concert, and I had not been invited. I stayed home all night, gloomy and dramatic, spending most of the evening in my room pouting. I was angry and crushed. It wasn't the first—or even close to the last—time I was not invited somewhere I wanted to be. But the memory of the sadness of exclusion has stayed with me.

The pain of not being invited to an event we want to go to, being excluded by a group of people we consider good friends, is not something we outgrow, despite growing out of the melodramas of adolescence. Human beings are social creatures—it's one of the reasons why solitary confinement is such a cruel and unusual punishment; we are made for community. God created us to be in communion with God's self but also with other human beings. The human psyche does not do well in the absence of other people.

We long to be invited even to events we have no desire to attend—simply because we want to be included. We want other people to desire our presence and involvement. Animals that evolve as social creatures do so because their species function best in groups; individual survival rates are improved by remaining with the group. As social creatures, humans are hardwired to be members of a group, and we never outgrow our desperate desire to belong. At one time or another, most of us have uttered the words, "I didn't *want to go. I* just wanted to be *invited.*" Sometimes it's not even about the event—it's just knowing that the invitation was there. My husband received some incredible professional football tickets through work, including access to an exclusive suite. I don't like football. It's not an antisports thing—I can speak for hours on something as simple as the art of the bunt in baseball or softball. I'm just not a football fan. So, when my husband asked if I wanted to go to the football game, I insisted he should take someone who would enjoy the game. He and his father had an amazing time. But I still appreciated that he offered the spot to me first. It feels good to be invited.

Exclusive Invitations

If you have ever participated in planning a wedding, you know how difficult extending invitations can be. There are some agonizing questions over who makes it onto the guest list. The list can be restricted by factors such as budget and venue size. There is great stress in compiling such a list because we may fear leaving someone out or offending someone who thought they should have been invited.

All too often, Christianity becomes an exclusive club that only certain people are allowed to enter. The list of ways Christianity has done this is extensive. I encountered it occasionally in my time as a campus minister. I once was "tabling" on campus—staffing a table set up in a prominent place to promote the ministry—when I was approached by a young man. He wanted to know what people had to believe to be a part of our campus ministry. I was a little bit baffled. Anyone was welcome to come to our ministry events. There was no "belief" requirement to participate. I expected that people in attendance would treat one another with respect and kindness, but no one had to sign a statement of belief to attend worship or activities.

I wasn't quite sure where he was coming from, but as the conversation progressed, I could sense that he was attempting to lay the groundwork for some sort of argument—his questions had an edge of accusation rather than curiosity. And sure enough, he quickly began lecturing me on our group's "lack of real Christian values." He insisted that everyone in the ministry should be required to sign a statement of belief; how else could I, as the pastor, make sure they were "real Christians"? I tried to tell him that measuring an individual's relationship with the Divine is God's job, not mine. Eventually, we circled back around to my insistence that "everyone is invited and welcome," which was the statement he found so problematic, most likely because he came from a Christian tradition more concerned with exclusion than with inclusion.

And this is the beauty of God's invitation to us, and God's invitation that we are compelled to share with others: everyone is on the guest list. Unlike the limited guest list for a wedding or party, every-one is invited to God's kin-dom. There are no budget factors; there are no space restrictions; there are no complex factors to consider; there are no exclusions from God's love.

Invited to Participate

Of the twelve texts that compose the readings from Hebrew Scriptures during Advent in the Revised Common Lectionary, eleven are con-cerned with or directly address the exile of the people of Israel. Along with the exodus from Egypt, Israel's seventy years of exile in Babylon is one of the defining communal memories of the Jewish people.

Our culture has not accustomed us to think of the pre-Christmas season and exile as subjects that go hand in hand, but the theme of exile in Advent is embedded deep within the Christian tradition. Con-sider the lyrics to "O Come, O Come, Emmanuel": "O come, O come, Emmanuel, / and ransom captive Israel, / that mourns in lonely exile here / until the Son of God appear." These lyrics were translated from Latin into English by John Mason Neale in the mid-nineteenth cen-tury, from a hymn based on a series of antiphons that had been written by monastics in the eighth or ninth century.[2]

The theme of longing for home and homecoming, a longing to be right with God and reside in the comfort of the homeland once again, is common among the exilic texts. The theme of exile also highlights to us the need for a savior; it leads up to the Christmas story with how desperately the people were longing for a messiah, the one who would both save (rescue them from harm) and deliver (set them free). The lectionary throughout the season of Advent is making a strong argument for the need for the Messiah; in Christianity we interpret this as the need for Jesus, and therefore for all of humanity's need for Christmas.

At the time of the prophet Jeremiah, the Jewish people were not in need of a party, but they were in desperate need of hope. The prophet extends an invitation to hope and goes on to list reasons that the peo-ple ought to accept the invitation. Although the text from Jeremiah has a lighter and more hopeful ring than the text from Luke, Jeremi-ah's proclamation of hope is set in one of Israel's most dire moments.

After the reign of King Solomon, Israel divided into the northern kingdom of Israel and the southern kingdom of Judah. The northern kingdom fell to the Assyrians, and the people of Judah lived in fear of being conquered as well for over a century. Although most biblical scholars maintain that Jeremiah was written in the exilic era, the narrative of Jeremiah locates itself around the fall of Jerusalem. Jeremiah's prophetic announcement in chapter 33 recalls the moments when the armies of Babylon were encroaching on Jerusalem, with no hope for victory in sight. Shortly after this declaration (another doomsday prophecy that angered the authorities) Jeremiah would be imprisoned by King Zedekiah, Jerusalem would fall, the streets would be littered with dead, and most of the survivors of this onslaught would be forced to live in exile in Babylon. These are not intended as words for a people on the eve of a great victory; rather, they are words delivered to a people hovering on the doorstep of devastation.

Therefore, in the midst of destruction and desolation, Jeremiah's words suggest even more hope than we might first perceive from our twenty-first-century perspective. In Jeremiah 33:15, we read, "In those days and at that time I will cause a righteous Branch to spring up for David; and he shall execute justice and righteousness in the land." While the familial line of King David has been cut down, Jeremiah prophesies that a branch may yet still grow from the stump. Jeremiah's words assure the people that even though they feel abandoned, God is still with them. Jeremiah goes on, "In those days Judah will be saved and Jerusalem will live in safety" (v. 16). Despite all evidence to the contrary, they will survive, and even thrive, on the other end of these horrific events. Jeremiah's prophecy is an invitation to hope, even when hope seems futile. It is an invitation to believe that God will prevail, an invitation to trust that God is not finished yet. It is an invitation to be a part of the work that God is still doing in the world and to be active participants in the ongoing kin-dom of God.

Active Waiting

Jeremiah invites people to be a part of the ongoing kin-dom building that God is doing in the world, and Jesus' words in this week's Gospel passage also offer invitation to remain active participants in the kin-dom work of God. Throughout the history of human thought, people around the world have repeatedly asked similar questions about ethics, morality, and the origins of the universe. Almost every culture or religion has a story of how humankind began, and in a similar fashion, most cultures and religions tell stories about how humankind will end. Christianity's approach to the world's end is far more complicated than its approach to its creation. Throughout the past two millennia, many traditions within Christianity have placed heavy significance on the *eschaton* (end times), an area of study that theologians refer to as *eschatology*. Scriptures concerned with the end times and the second coming of Jesus are cryptic, mysterious, and complicated.

Within my own tradition, I have rarely encountered much interest about the return of Jesus or the end times. I know that my denomination is not alone in this phenomenon. We shy away from speaking of such topics in fear of being confused with those we consider more radical, or even extremist. But we cannot ignore a text just because it makes us ask uncomfortable questions. Indeed, my tradition's liturgy for the sacrament of Holy Communion addresses the return of Jesus with these words: "Christ has died. Christ has risen. Christ will come again."

Luke 21 makes clear that the return of Jesus will not be a time of contentment and rest for all people. "Signs in the sun, the moon, and the stars, and on the earth distress among nations confused by the roaring of the sea and the waves. People will faint from fear and foreboding of what is coming upon the world, for the powers of the heavens will be shaken" (vv. 25–26). That sounds terrifying! These are not soothing words of comfort; I think it is safe to say that no one will be turning Luke 21 into a lullaby anytime soon. It is easy to wonder why we begin the season of Advent with a scriptural focus on the end of the world. However, Advent is a season in which we are preparing our hearts, minds, and souls for the coming of Christ in the past, present, and future. If we think of Advent in these terms, it makes sense that we begin the season with Scriptures that evoke the final coming of Christ in the future.

However, throughout the ages, some Christians have clung to these eschatological passages with unhealthy fervor. They have obsessed over predicting the end of the world, looking to political and natural phenomena around the world to back up their predictions. Many have done so to the point of eschewing their responsibilities as people of God. It is important to remember that many predictions have been made over the past two millennia of the date and time Jesus will return—and to date, all of them have been incorrect. On the opposite end of this obsession with the apocalypse, sometimes Christianity has painted a safer version of Jesus, the one who holds a lamb and says only, "Let the children come to me." Some people prefer this safer version of Jesus who does not say such frightening things about heaven and earth passing away. But if we are going to dive into Scripture, we cannot shy away from its complexities, and we cannot simply omit Jesus' words because they cause discomfort.

There is danger in focusing on Jesus' words of warning, because we risk giving up the hard work for change and justice in the world. If the world is ending tomorrow, why bother? There is also danger in softening Jesus and ignoring Scripture that makes us uncomfortable; we risk losing the drive to action when we lose Jesus' message of immediacy. The faithful Christian is called to find a middle ground between these two approaches, to seek out a both-and approach to living out the commands of these texts. We are called to live into the knowledge that Jesus could return at any moment but also live into the hard work of seeking to make God's kin-dom a reality here on earth, because that return may be thousands of years in the distant future.

Jesus tells his followers in this passage to be alert for the second coming. His words contain an invitation: be alert, for the earthly realm is not eternal. But there are different sorts of waiting. There is the waiting we do in a waiting room when a loved one is having surgery. There is the waiting we do when we are in stand-still traffic. There is the waiting we do when a colleague is late to a scheduled appointment. But all of these are a passive sort of waiting. I cannot speed up the surgeon's hands, clean up the accident ahead of me on the highway, or hurry along a colleague who is running behind. Instead, Jesus calls us to a different sort of waiting. This is waiting in an active sense, where the focus is on preparation and anticipation. It is the waiting we do when we excitedly prepare for a beloved guest to arrive in our homes.

In my childhood home, the stairs to the second floor provided an excellent place to sit and wait with full view of the front door and the driveway. I remember sitting and waiting on those steps on many occasions—for a ride, for the bus, but I especially remember the anticipation of sitting and waiting on those steps for the expected arrival of grandparents or visiting friends. As an adult, I am usually waiting for the arrival of guests by doing all the things that I just haven't yet finished: wiping down the kitchen counters one last time, tidying up the kitchen table, making sure that beds are made and fresh towels are available, putting the final touches on something I'm preparing in the kitchen. I had the childhood luxury of passively waiting for visitors, but the adult form of waiting for loved ones to arrive usually involves a great deal of action.

In the same way, being alert does not mean hunkering down in bunkers and waiting for the end. Instead, we wait as people called to continue to do the good work of Jesus Christ until the last moment we are able. Jesus invites us to work for the inbreaking of God's reign on earth. Like most invitations, Jesus' requires a response. But this response goes far beyond a simple yes or no. The invitation is to be a participant, not merely a bystander.

Come as You Are

In stark contrast with the young man who was offended by a ministry that invited anyone to come in, around that same time a young woman contacted me privately via social media, asking, "What do I have to believe to come to your ministry?" I happily responded, "You don't have to believe anything. Our only expectation is that participants show one another respect." She responded to the invitation with active participation and became so involved that she eventually joined our leadership team. Later, I would ask what drew her to our ministry. She told me that our ministry's slogan that year, "Come as You Are," had intrigued her. She found that invitation welcoming and nonjudgmental, suggesting that perhaps the ministry was a safe place where she could do the hard work to figure out her own beliefs without pressure; maybe this was a safe place to ask a lot of questions. She stayed because that's exactly what she found.

We all want to be invited. There is something within each of us that wants to be included. We want to be invited to the table, to the party, to join the club. When I have finished the liturgy of the Great Thanksgiving and blessed the cup and the bread for Communion, I always get a little giddy when it is time to remind everyone of my favorite part of being a United Methodist: we do not believe the Table belongs to us. When we offer Communion in a United Methodist setting, anyone who wants to follow Jesus is welcome to receive Communion, regardless of membership status in any church. I have the opportunity to extend this invitation each time I preside over the sacrament: "If you seek to follow Jesus, you are welcome to receive Communion here—regardless of your membership in this or any other church."

Growing up, I experienced a variety of traditions through attending religious services with friends: Roman Catholic mass, vacation Bible school in other Protestant traditions, Mormon youth group, and worship services at an Orthodox church and a synagogue. As a child, I accepted that these faiths were different from my own, and because I was not part of their community, there were certain things from which I would be excluded in worship.

But by the time I had gone through confirmation and begun some intensive Bible study, I understood a lot more than I had earlier in my childhood. In some cases, I struggled more with the exclusion I experienced in these services. I remember a specific occasion when I attended church with one of my friends in my teenage years. I knew before attending the service that when it came time for Communion, I could not receive Communion because I was not a member of their denomination. This had not bothered me prior to the service. Unfortunately, on that day, the clergyperson's message centered around celebrating how the Communion table "unites Christians around the world." He kept using "Christian," and all I could think of was the character Inigo Montoya from *Princess Bride,* who said, "You keep using that word; I do not think it means what you think it means." I was a Christian! So why was I not welcome at this table that allegedly united Christians from around the world? I felt the blood rising in my cheeks and my hands began to clench. How dare he say that all Christians were united in this meal, when I was expected to remain in my seat?

While my own denomination is riddled with extensive flaws of its own, I enthusiastically embrace our theological belief that the Table is for anyone wanting to follow Christ. Because being invited matters. Invitation is the beginning. The places where heaven and earth meet are often referred to as "thin spaces." The thin space I experience through Communion allows me a glimpse of God's kin-dom. So, when I have the privilege of blessing the cup and bread, I feel like I am throwing a joyous and elaborate celebration, and I get the privilege of inviting everyone present; on God's behalf, I get to invite everyone to the best party in all of creation. We are invited to "come as we are" to the Communion celebration where we meet Jesus over and over again at the Table to experience God's extravagant grace.

Jesus doesn't want us to cower in fear when we meet him. On the contrary, he says, "Stand up and raise your heads, because your redemption is drawing near." This is an invitation to stand tall with the confidence of a child of God—whatever may come. We are invited to wait for Jesus this Advent season, to stand alert, and we are invited to participate in the difficult and holy work of creating God's kin-dom here on earth. Jesus is coming, ready or not. How will you invite Christ to come this Advent season?

QUESTIONS FOR REFLECTION AND DISCUSSION

1. What does it feel like to be left off the guest list? Recall a time when you were not invited to an event you wanted to attend. How did you feel? How did you handle the situation? Why do you still remember it?
2. Consider an invitation that changed your life, or an invitation that put you in the right place at the right time. Who offered the invitation? How did receiving the invitation change you or the path you took? Why did you respond to the invitation?
3. What is the meaning of "kin-dom," and how might its use differ from the more traditional usage of "kingdom"? How might kin-dom language influence who feels invited to the Table when we consider all of God's people?
4. We can respond to God's invitation by extending invitations of our own. How will you invite others to participate in God's kin-dom this Advent season? By inviting others to worship, to Bible study, or into your home or by making it clear that everyone is invited to the Table?

5. How will you extend hospitality in the season as we prepare for the arrival of Jesus in the past, present, and future?
6. What is the difference between passive waiting and active waiting? How is Advent a season of active waiting?
7. How can you respond to the invitations contained in Scripture this week? How are you being called to actively participate in the ongoing building of God's kin-dom?

Find the companion video for week one of Advent at http://tiny.cc /StayAwhileSession1.

DAILY REFLECTIONS

Monday

While working on *Stay Awhile,* I often listened to Sara Groves's song "Every Minute" from her 2002 album *All Right Here.* In the song, she sings about gathering with family and friends. The song is available on multiple streaming platforms, including YouTube. Take some time to listen to the song today and contemplate how it speaks to hospitality as a spiritual act. How might these themes of hospitality help prepare your soul for the season of Advent?

Tuesday

I was unpacking boxes in my dorm room in Woods Hall when a girl from down the hall came by to introduce herself. She saw me unpacking my Bible and *The United Methodist Hymnal* I had been gifted from my home church, and she excitedly told me she was also a United Methodist. She invited me to join her when she went to the Wesley House for dinner the next day. I had planned on exploring other faith traditions through my college years. Did I really want to be Methodist? That's how I was raised, but what else was out there? Although I went to a lot of other campus ministries in those first few months (one of which even asked me not to return), I kept coming back to the Wesley House. That first casual invitation drew me in, but the hospitality I felt there kept me coming back. It felt like going home.

Where are places that have felt like home for you? What makes a space feel like home? How does this impact your understanding of hospitality? How might this impact your journey as you prepare your heart and mind for the coming of Christ in the past, present, and future?

Wednesday

As an adult, when I check my physical mailbox, I usually expect to find bills and lots of advertisements. With the exceptions of Christmas and birthdays, most mail I receive is boring—at best. But when I received mail as a child, it was a special occasion, because most of the time, it was an invitation. In the days before texting, social media, and evites, this was how we invited one another to attend birthday parties—by sending invitations through the mail. Parents today assure me that this is mostly of a bygone era, but during my childhood years, there was something special about receiving the invitation.

In addition to saying that you were invited, the invitations sometimes hinted at what the theme of the party was going to be. One year I had an ocean-themed birthday party complete with a trip to the local pool and an orca piñata and birthday cake. My invitations to that year's party had an ocean theme. My friends could anticipate what the party would be like, based on that invitation.

Remember the most recent invitation you have received—by mail, text, email. What did it tell you about the event you were invited to attend? What did it convey about the event itself? Use today to consider the invitations contained in Sunday's Scripture. What do they tell us about God? What do they tell us about those who worship God?

Thursday

Within the vast array of vampire myth, there is a long-standing tradition that a vampire cannot enter a person's home unless it receives an invitation. These myths tend to maintain that the threshold of a home holds magical or sacred power, and so an invitation across the threshold contains a great deal of power. What power can you wield with invitations in your own life? How might you use invitations for building God's kin-dom?

Friday

I learned at an early age that on Halloween night, houses with lit-up front porches are inviting kids to trick-or-treat, and houses with no lights should be skipped. As excited children, we understandably wanted to ring the bell and get candy at every house on the block, but adults taught us that it was rude to ring the bell if the front porch lights were not on. Lights off meant we were not invited—the residents were either not home or not passing out candy.

In the first house my husband and I owned, we usually had more than one hundred trick-or-treaters on Halloween. One Halloween, we purchased our candy and put it in a bowl beside the front door. We then turned on a movie and began waiting for trick-or-treaters to ring the doorbell. About an hour after dark, we realized no one had come to our house. Confused, we looked out the front windows to see dozens of children and parents parading through our cul-de-sac, going from one house to the next. But they were all skipping our house. We suddenly realized we had forgotten to turn on the front porch lights!

On Halloween, the flick of a light switch can provide an invitation. What visible signs in your home or faith community tell people they are invited? What are ways that you can make a space or building more inviting for others? We know that God invites us to be a part of a great cloud of believers, so how can we make sure others receive the invitation?

Saturday

Will I have a place at the table?
What if I sit down, and inside they all laugh.
They might know I am a fraud, a fake, an imposter.
They might see through the manicured presentation;
I might slip and let them see what I really am.
If they see me, will I still be allowed to sit?

What if I sit down and accidentally spill
my sorrow and shame all over the tablecloth,
and they drip down off the table onto the floor?
Those seated before me might see my scars,
hide their disgust between knowing glances,
lose their appetites, and excuse themselves,
leaving me seated at this long table,
alone.
They might see my hideous rage, my calloused indifference,
my self-pity and self-doubt, all the broken pieces.
Will they still break bread with me?

Second Sunday of Advent

PLAN

Jeremiah 29:5–14; Mark 1:1–8

Build houses and live in them; plant gardens and eat what they produce. Take wives and have sons and daughters; take wives for your sons, and give your daughters in marriage, that they may bear sons and daughters; multiply there, and do not decrease. But seek the welfare of the city where I have sent you into exile, and pray to the LORD on its behalf, for in its welfare you will find your welfare. For thus says the LORD of hosts, the God of Israel: Do not let the prophets and the diviners who are among you deceive you, and do not listen to the dreams that they dream, for it is a lie that they are prophesying to you in my name; I did not send them, says the LORD.

For thus says the LORD: Only when Babylon's seventy years are completed will I visit you, and I will fulfill to you my promise and bring you back to this place. For surely I know the plans I have for you, says the LORD, plans for your welfare and not for harm, to give you a future with hope. Then when you call upon me and come and pray to me, I will hear you. When you search for me, you will find me; if you seek me with all your heart, I will let you find me, says the LORD, and I will restore your fortunes and gather you from all the nations and all the places where I have driven you, says the LORD, and I will bring you back to the place from which I sent you into exile.

Jeremiah 29:5–14

The beginning of the good news of Jesus Christ, the Son of God.
As it is written in the prophet Isaiah,

"See, I am sending my messenger ahead of you,
who will prepare your way;
the voice of one crying out in the wilderness:
'Prepare the way of the Lord,
make his paths straight,'"

John the baptizer appeared in the wilderness, proclaiming a baptism of repentance for the forgiveness of sins. And people from the whole Judean countryside and all the people of Jerusalem were going out to him, and were baptized by him in the river Jordan, confessing their sins. Now John was clothed with camel's hair, with a leather belt around his waist, and he ate locusts and wild honey. He proclaimed, "The one who is more powerful than I is coming after me; I am not worthy to stoop down and untie the thong of his sandals. I have baptized you with water; but he will baptize you with the Holy Spirit."

Mark 1:1–8

*I*n both the secular and the religious realms, I usually begin planning for Christmas around the end of October. This is mostly a result of how packed a clergyperson's calendar can look in December, attempting to fulfill both personal and professional obligations. I learned long ago that I will enjoy the Advent and Christmas seasons more if I have plans in place far in advance—whether that means finishing my liturgy for Christmas Eve by the beginning of November or having Christmas presents for family and friends purchased and wrapped by Thanksgiving Day. If I want to enjoy the secular and religious parts of Christmas, it requires planning in advance.

Planning is necessary in the realm of hospitality. Plans are required for venue, food, beverages, accommodations, decorations, and the list goes on. In the case of weddings, some people plan so far in advance that they send out a round of save-the-date cards prior to the actual invitations. Through Advent, we look to how God's salvific plan changed with the birth of Jesus Christ and how we can make plans to engage the ongoing work of creating God's kin-dom here on earth.

Because the words "plan" and "prepare" are often used inter-changeably, it is important to distinguish how they are used for the purposes of the themes of this devotional. I use the theme of "plan" to refer to the mental work that occurs prior to offering hospital-ity, while I am using "prepare" (next week's theme) to refer to the action and physical activities that take place to prepare for an event. We will explore how these themes can play out differently in our spiritual lives during the anticipatory season of Advent.

Better than Whatever

In 2009, a reality show called *Chopped* began airing on the Food Network. The premise of the show is that four chefs are given a bas-ket with four ingredients, and the chefs are tasked with preparing a dish with the basket ingredients plus what they can find in a well-stocked pantry. Watching the chefs think on their feet to plan and cook a dish for the judges is part of the appeal of the show, because professional chefs usually have much more time to consider their ingredients and what they will prepare. In normal circumstances, chefs have time to plan.

Sometimes, when my husband and I begin discussing what we will have for dinner, especially following a busy day at work, we settle on "whatever." This means we each will scrounge up our own meal from whatever is in the freezer, pantry, and fridge. "Whatever" meals at our house are less elegant than those presented by profes-sional chefs on *Chopped,* but the idea is the same—work with what we've got and eat what's at hand.

But when we know guests are coming, we don't just sniff the roast chicken from last week to make sure it's still edible. Careful planning goes into the event—plans for cleaning and tidying, but especially for meal planning. The more complicated the preparation, and the more mouths to feed, the more planning is required to get food to the table.

While many people in my life have shown me spectacular examples of hospitality, one of my favorite guides is Anne Edwards, a fictional character. Author Mary Doria Russell created Anne, an anthropolo-gist turned physician, as a character in her novel *The Sparrow*. Anne is constantly hosting other people in the home she shares with her husband, George, and it is how Anne plans for these events that is remarkable. She plans her menus around what will make her guests feel the most at home. She consults with a Puerto Rican friend to learn to make bacalaitos for a Puerto Rican guest, tackles multiple recipes for Texas barbecue when hosting a priest from Texas, and on another occasion plans her menu around the ancestry of a Sephardic Jewish guest from Turkey.

Anne loves to make guests feel welcome in her home, but none of her culinary attempts at hospitality are spontaneous. She spends a lot of time thinking through the menu, searching for ingredients, and considering what will please her guests the most. Anne does a lot of planning.

When my husband and I are planning a special dinner for guests, one of the first things to consider is the menu—what will we serve? One of the first places to begin is in asking, What do our guests enjoy? My mother hates the flavor of coffee, so if she is coming, there will be no coffee flavors in the dessert. When my sister comes for dinner, cheese is always a win for an appetizer. If my friend Courtney is coming, I know we'll have chocolate for dessert.

Because the goal is to please the guests, we don't just serve "whatever" for dinner. There are many considerations beyond the preferences of our guests, like what is in season, what ingredients are available, how much time it takes to prepare a dish, and how much food needs to be prepared. I'm not going to serve strawberry shortcake—where strawberries are the star of the dish—in January. The strawberries aren't going to be very good. I'm also not going to prepare a turkey dinner on a random Thursday after work.

Because nothing appears on the table by magic, planning is vital to the process. Anyone who has hosted a large family gathering can attest to the amount of planning that goes into even the simplest of holiday celebrations when there are many guests to feed. How many people are coming? Where will they sit? Do we have enough tables, chairs, plates, and so on? While I would admittedly have few objections, most people would be disappointed to discover that lunch at a large family gathering will consist of just turkey and desserts. So we also need to ask, Who is bringing which food items? Planning is vital to the work of hospitality.

Potluck Hospitality

While planning the food is a vital element of hospitality, planning how to utilize a space is also important, and making a space hospitable can vary depending on the space and the event. Every summer, I volunteer at a high school summer camp, and I am assigned to a classroom on a college campus that will be my group's meeting place for the week. Trying to turn a college classroom into a welcoming space is no simple feat. In addition to my own luggage for the week, I usually pack so many supplies for camp that there is barely space for me in my car. Part of the supplies consist of blankets and pillows to spread out on the floor of my group's assigned room, items that will make our week more comfortable in an otherwise not-so-comfortable space. I usually add some handmade posters or other decorations that go with the theme of the week. My supplies also include items like colorful streamers and Christmas lights, items to hang around the room and transform it into something cozier than the cold four walls of a classroom. There is a magical feel during evening sessions when we turn off the overhead fluorescent lights and meet by the glow of the Christmas lights.

In recent years, however, I've stopped spending so much time decorating our space before the campers arrive. Instead, our first group activity is decorating the room together. This strategy might seem counterintuitive to planning a hospitable environment, as it seems as if the goal ought to be the creation of a welcoming setting upon a guest's arrival. However, I have learned that letting the group decorate the room together serves multiple purposes, the most important being that it gives them an investment in the space—the camaraderie of feeling like "this space belongs to *us*."

It is in this vein that I have also come to understand something important about planning and hospitality—my favorite form of hospitality to receive is what I call potluck hospitality. While more formal forms of hospitality might include a greeting at the door and an offer to take the guest's coat while a drink is prepared, I am less comfortable with the formality of this sort of introduction into someone's home. The hospitality I am most comfortable receiving is the potluck kind, where I get to contribute and participate when I arrive. I love when friends ask me to keep an eye on what's in the oven or to stand at the stove and stir while they set the table. Being handed a familiar task sets me at ease more quickly than the warmest of welcomes. Having someone prepare a drink for you sends the message that you are a valued guest; but being invited to pour your own drink? That is a message that you are home. The beauty of potluck hospitality is allowing guests to contribute to the event, giving them the opportunity to feel invested, and even at home.

Not according to the Plan

In March 2020, most churches closed, and nearly everyone had to cancel plans. Due to COVID-19, plans that had been in place for years were tabled, sometimes rescheduled multiple times before being canceled altogether; life as we knew it seemed to come to a standstill. Despite the disruption in humankind's stability and routine, however, the grass still grew, the buds still appeared, our chicks still grew into chickens, and the seeds took root and sprouted in the garden. Nature had a plan all its own, and no one had informed it that anything had been canceled. It was an important reminder in the midst of the loneliness and upheaval: the plan of creation was still intact; the order of the universe still worked. I found reassurance that, despite my plans being canceled, some plans were fully operational. The earth still spun, the planets still orbited, and the sun still shone.

So while there are always certain things we can rely on (the earth will spin, the planets will orbit, the sun will shine), we can also rely on the fact that something will always go differently than we have planned—because this is the unpredictable nature of life. We can prepare all we want, but sometimes things go awry, in both beautiful and terrible ways.

One of my duties as a pastor is to provide premarital counseling to couples, and one promise I make to all couples is that *at least* one thing will go wrong on their wedding day. The goal is not to frighten them or increase anxiety but to remind them that no matter how much effort and planning we put into something, life happens, and that the real purpose of the day is not the perfectly executed party or cake or flowers but the union of the marriage itself. A wedding day, like all other days, will not be perfect. Such is the nature of life.

This is the beauty we see in the Scripture passages for this week. Sometimes our plans fall apart, but God is always at work in creating something new. Planning is essential in both our spiritual and secular lives, but we must adapt and live in the reality that plans change as life changes around us. The prophet Jeremiah helps the Hebrew people adjust their plans as they attempt to navigate their new lives in Babylonian exile, and in the passage from Mark, we see how God works through Jesus Christ to make a new salvific plan for the entire world.

In the first week's text from Jeremiah, Judah's capital city of Jerusalem is about to be destroyed by the Babylonians. In this week's text, the nation of Judah—including Jerusalem—has already been conquered. When Babylon conquered other nations, they sent the defeated nation's strongest and most educated citizens to live in Babylon, thereby removing the people most likely to lead a rebellion and take back their homeland. So, after Judah is conquered, the best and brightest Judeans are forced to live in exile in Babylon. By the time we encounter this text in Jeremiah, the people's need for hope is high—the time for chastisement has passed, because their judgment has already swept down upon them.

Like last week's text, Jeremiah 29 addresses the Jewish people in Babylonian exile, who have been traumatized by devastation and loss; the prophet Jeremiah assures the doubting that God is still with them. Their doubt seems natural, given the state of things. The doubt that comes in moments of darkness is one shared by all humankind, across generations and centuries. While we may not have shared the exile's experience of losing our homeland, how many of us have shared in the experience of having a dark night of the soul? We all experience these moments in our lives—I know I certainly have. There are nights when it feels as if the sun will never rise again and my pillow will never dry from the tears I've shed. There have been times when I have felt certain that, if God existed at all, God was decidedly working against me. I imagine this is similar to what the people in exile felt, that their God had abandoned them.

It is easy to understand this feeling of abandonment when we look at the cultural context of the ancient world. At the time and place this passage is addressing, there was a common belief that is difficult for us to relate to from a twenty-first-century Western perspective.

In the ancient world, most cultures in the Middle East believed that if one army conquered another army, the conquering army's gods were more powerful than the losing army's gods. Switching one's loyalty to the gods of one's conquerors may have simply been self-preservation, but there was also theological logic in switching to gods that had (in their minds) proven more powerful than their own. If their gods couldn't protect them, perhaps the gods of the conquerors might? It was in line with the culture of the time for the people of Judah to believe that when they were conquered by the Babylonians, their god Yahweh was also conquered by Babylon's gods.

Furthermore, the ancient Hebrew people believed that Yahweh lived in the Holy of Holies in the temple in Jerusalem. They believed that the only place God could rightly be worshiped was in the temple in Jerusalem. The destruction of the temple destroyed not only their place of worship but also a foundational piece of their understanding of God. How and where could they faithfully worship? The defeat of their armies combined with the destruction of the temple required a complete reworking of their theology—fundamental restructuring of both their belief and practice.

It is within this framework of chaos and turmoil that Jeremiah tries to assure the people that God is still at work among them. In this passage, Jeremiah simultaneously assures the Jewish people of their future with God while also delivering the painful news that the exile is going to last for a while. Jeremiah's prophecy is God's way of calling the people to plant gardens, get married, and have children (Jer. 29:5–6); in other words, God orders them to go on with the ordinary tasks of living while they wait for their return to Israel. Verses 10 and 11 assure the people that their time in exile is not forever, that God has a beautiful future in mind for them. God has planned for the people's future, and they are called to active participation in this plan.

Unfortunately, verse 11 is often quoted out of context. "I know the plans I have for you, says the LORD, plans for your welfare and not for harm, to give you a future with hope." I have often heard it used as a verbal bandage on wounds that require stitches, a sort of unhelpful placation offered to someone in a bad situation. There is great danger when Scripture is removed from context or even when we attempt to sum up complex theology in false but pithy sentiments such as "God will never give you more than you can handle." This text in Jeremiah is not intended as a promise to assist individuals through difficult times, as it is so often misused. Rather, the text is a communal promise that God will never forget the covenant made with the people of Abraham and Sarah. The Jewish people in exile, despite the upheaval of their theology, their geography, and even their identity, are called to plan for the future. The plan may need to be adapted, but they are still called to plan.

A New Plan

Unlike the lengthy poetic prophecy frequently encountered in the Hebrew text, the Gospel of Mark is the shortest of the four Gospels. Most scholars agree that Mark was the first Gospel of our canon to be written, and it seems likely that the writers of both Matthew and Luke had access to Mark's Gospel when writing their own accounts. Unlike the other Gospels, Mark is known for brevity and does not spend any time on Jesus' origins. Mark's attitude is to get straight to the main course, cut the appetizers and the amuse-bouche, no frills or fancy presentation, just bring on the meat! There is something to be said for this abrupt approach; Mark certainly gets straight to the point.

It is possible the author was conveying Jesus' life in a style common to Scriptures about the calling of the Hebrew prophets. (Most Hebrew prophets have a call story, two examples being Isa. 6:1–13 and Jer. 1:4–19.) In *Social World of the Hebrew Prophets,* Victor Matthews writes concerning these call stories, "The intention of the stories is to confer authority on the prophet, not to provide biographical information."[3] Matthews notes that the literary patterns in these stories include theophany (divine encounter), introductory word or greeting, and a sign empowering the person who has been chosen. Although Matthews is writing strictly of the Hebrew prophets, the author of Mark follows the same narrative guidelines in constructing this concise Gospel. Mark is establishing the authority of both John the baptizer and Jesus from Nazareth as quickly as possible for the reader of the Gospel.

Mark draws direct parallels between John the Baptist and the prophet Elijah. Second Kings 1:8 describes Elijah as "a hairy man, with a leather belt around his waist." This sounds a lot like John the Baptist, whom Mark describes as "clothed with camel's hair, with a leather belt around his waist." The drawing of this parallel designates John as a prophet in the style of the Hebrew Scriptures. Mark also quotes Isaiah 40 directly, "prepare the way of the LORD," making further use of the Hebrew Scriptures to confirm that the coming of Jesus Christ is part of God's plan to fulfill the promises God has made to the children of Abraham. While Mark does not spend excess time on frills, he does use this framing from the Hebrew Scriptures to set the stage for his presentation of John the Baptist. John's ministry helps prepare the way for the Lord. Ready or not, God is coming; the themes of the urgency and immediacy of the coming kin-dom of God are woven throughout Mark.

It is also significant that Mark sets Jesus' baptism in the Jordan River. (Remember, Mark is never careless in his use of words— every word is intentional.) The crossing of the Jordan River in Joshua 3 marked the establishment of Israel after the Hebrew people had wandered in the wilderness for forty years. Mark's use of the Jordan River indicates that God is establishing a new salvific plan on the banks of the river.

This new plan of salvation—enacted through the life, teaching, death, and resurrection of Jesus—offers God's grace to all people. John Wesley, the founder of the Methodist movement, wrote a great deal about prevenient grace, the grace God has laid out for us before we even know it is available. God's extension of hospitality in this grace evokes a response from us, calling us to extend that grace and hospitality to others. The hymn "Come, Sinners, to the Gospel Feast," written by Charles Wesley, centers around this doctrine of prevenient grace: "Come, sinners, to the gospel feast; / let every soul be Jesus' guest. / Ye need not one be left behind, / for God hath bid all humankind. // . . . The invitation is to all."[4] God has already planned out the feast of grace; prevenient grace is how we are able to respond to the plan and invitation.

In Advent, we are anticipating the coming of Christ in the past, present, and future. So how do we plan for the coming of Christ? Because our plan for welcoming Jesus (and welcoming those who seek to follow him) ought to be better than "whatever." Praying, journaling, meditating, reading Scripture, worshiping, and listening to music are all ways we can explore and plan how we will help to build God's kin-dom. Because in God's kin-dom, we aren't just planning for those who are already in the house. We are planning for those who have not yet come to the Table, for those who do not even know that they are longing to receive the meal. We are planning to set at liberty those who are oppressed, release the captives, and comfort those who mourn, as Jesus proclaims. We are preparing for peace. And these aren't the sorts of things that happen overnight. This takes careful planning. This Advent, how can we plan for those who are not yet at the Table?

QUESTIONS FOR REFLECTION AND DISCUSSION

1. Describe a time you have participated in extensive planning. What was the event or occasion? How long did it take to plan? How much effort went into the plans?
2. When you are a guest, are you more comfortable becoming part of the planned event or being an observer? Why? Does this come from your culture or your personality?
3. Describe a plan that was disrupted in your life when the COVID-19 pandemic caused shutdowns in March 2020. Were you able to adjust the plans? If you were unable to reschedule, how did you feel?
4. What does it mean for the Jewish people in exile that they have been tasked with making plans in exile? Why would this be a challenge for them? When was a time when you needed to adjust a major plan in your life? What did you learn?
5. The writer of the Gospel of Mark sets the stage for God to put a new plan in action through Jesus Christ. What makes this new covenant different from the old one?
6. What is your understanding of grace in your tradition? How does your understanding of grace impact your understanding of God's plans for humankind?
7. How can you be a part of planning for those not yet at the Table? What plans can you help enact to make space for those who have not yet responded to grace?

Find the companion video for week two of Advent at http://tiny.cc /StayAwhileSession2.

DAILY REFLECTIONS

Monday

Listen to the hymn "Come, Sinners, to the Gospel Feast." Versions of this song are available on multiple streaming platforms, including YouTube. Charles Wesley wrote the song about the theological concept of prevenient grace—the grace that goes before us before we know it exists. What do the lyrics of the song have to say about this understanding of grace? How does the song invite you to participate in God's plan of salvation? What is it like to know you can participate by extending invitations to other people? If you are musically inclined, play the song on your instrument or sing along.

Tuesday

In the introduction, I wrote about thin spaces—those times in life when the space between heaven and earth grows so thin that we can feel heaven's presence. Rarely have I encountered these thin spaces by accident. While on occasion I accidentally bump into one (chalk one up to prevenient grace), elements of planning or preparation usually go into these encounters with thin spaces in God's kin-dom. While we cannot plan thin spaces, we can plan events that might create them. Have you experienced a thin space in your own life? What was it like? How might you lay the groundwork for another similar experience?

Wednesday

When I served in campus ministry, we didn't have a building near campus. We had a single classroom at a local church. Even though we worshiped in the student union, many events took place in my home. Four years in a row I prepared an elaborate meal in my home during Holy Week. My final year in campus ministry, I hosted twenty-six people in my living room/kitchen. My husband and I lived in our starter house at the time, and hosting this many people required removing all our living room furniture to make space for tables. We borrowed tables, chairs, plates, and silverware from the local church and crammed everything into our home. Despite having moved out all the furniture, it was still a very tight squeeze.

Preparing an elaborate meal for twenty-six people in a regular household kitchen is no simple feat. It required extensive planning, coordination, and preparation. We had a standard kitchen with four regular burners and one oven. In the days leading up to the meal, figuring out how to fit everything in the refrigerator required every last ounce of the Tetris skills I had garnered in my youth.

Consider a time when you have had to plan extensively for an event. What was required of you, how did it go, and what did you learn? As we continue to plan for the coming of Christ in the past, present, and future, how are you preparing your heart, mind, and soul?

Thursday

One professor in seminary insisted that his students memorize the entire liturgy for Communion out of my denomination's hymnal. The entirety of the quiz was to come to class, write down the entire liturgy from memory, and turn in our work. At the time, with so much academic pressure on my plate, I believed this was a complete waste of my time. Why did I need to memorize something I could just read off a page? Worship isn't a theater performance.

Years later, I would write that professor an apology and thank him for his wisdom. A few weeks after my ordination, I was volunteering at church camp with more than one hundred youth. We had scheduled worship at a church near camp and had moved everything downstairs to the basement due to the weather forecast for the evening. A huge thunderstorm moved into the area during worship. I had been asked to preside over Communion, and around the time I stood up to walk to the front of the worship space, the power went out. A collective gasp went up as we were suddenly left in the dark, with more than 130 youth and adults in the room. I continued walking to the front. The only light we had in the room was the light of the exit signs (certainly not enough to read by), but I luckily had every word of the Communion liturgy memorized. The service went on as scheduled.

I was prepared for unforeseen contingencies thanks to my professor insisting I plan ahead. Can you think of a time when careful planning prepared you for unpredictable events in your own life? How were you grateful for careful planning when things went sideways? How can we utilize this lesson in our spiritual lives? How does God's planning look when our plans fall apart?

Friday

Planning is important in the Christian life, and it is also important in the kitchen. Things must be done in a certain order, and planning those steps is important. Potatoes must be washed, peeled, cooked, then mashed. Yes, technically you could peel them after they are cooked, but they certainly can't be mashed before they are cooked. When I'm making a dessert from a recipe that says, "Fold in the beaten egg whites," I can guarantee that the recipe isn't going to be successful if I skip the step where I beat the egg whites.

Consider the order to God's plan for our salvation. What does it mean that Jesus came into the world and lived among us? What does it mean that Jesus had to die on a cross and be resurrected for Christians to be saved? How might the good news of Christmas be viewed when we keep in mind what will take place during Holy Week next spring?

Saturday

How do you go about planning when you extend hospitality? What mental work do you find essential prior to hosting others? Do you write out grocery lists, make to-do lists, set out recipes? How do you think through using your space, from where people will sit to what will occupy the oven? What considerations need to be made for a gathering, be it for family or friends?

Consider writing out your own spiritual plan today. As you continue to prepare your heart, mind, and soul for the coming of Christ, how can you plan to keep the spirit of Christmas alive past December 25?

Third Sunday of Advent

PREPARE

Isaiah 61:1–4, 8–11; John 1:6–8, 19–28

The spirit of the Lord GOD is upon me,
    because the LORD has anointed me;
he has sent me to bring good news to the oppressed,
    to bind up the brokenhearted,
to proclaim liberty to the captives,
    and release to the prisoners;
to proclaim the year of the LORD's favor,
    and the day of vengeance of our God;
    to comfort all who mourn;
to provide for those who mourn in Zion—
    to give them a garland instead of ashes,
the oil of gladness instead of mourning,
    the mantle of praise instead of a faint spirit.
They will be called oaks of righteousness,
    the planting of the LORD, to display his glory.
They shall build up the ancient ruins,
    they shall raise up the former devastations;
they shall repair the ruined cities,
    the devastations of many generations.
. . . .
For I the LORD love justice,
    I hate robbery and wrongdoing;
I will faithfully give them their recompense,
    and I will make an everlasting covenant with them.
Their descendants shall be known among the nations,
    and their offspring among the peoples;
all who see them shall acknowledge
    that they are a people whom the LORD has blessed.

I will greatly rejoice in the LORD,
 my whole being shall exult in my God;
for he has clothed me with the garments of salvation,
 he has covered me with the robe of righteousness,
as a bridegroom decks himself with a garland,
 and as a bride adorns herself with her jewels.
For as the earth brings forth its shoots,
 and as a garden causes what is sown in it to spring up,
so the Lord GOD will cause righteousness and praise
 to spring up before all the nations.

Isaiah 61:1–4, 8–11

There was a man sent from God, whose name was John. He came as a witness to testify to the light, so that all might believe through him. He himself was not the light, but he came to testify to the light. . . .

This is the testimony given by John when the Jews sent priests and Levites from Jerusalem to ask him, "Who are you?" He confessed and did not deny it, but confessed, "I am not the Messiah." And they asked him, "What then? Are you Elijah?" He said, "I am not." "Are you the prophet?" He answered, "No." Then they said to him, "Who are you? Let us have an answer for those who sent us. What do you say about yourself?" He said,

"I am the voice of one crying out in the wilderness,
 'Make straight the way of the Lord,' "

as the prophet Isaiah said.

Now they had been sent from the Pharisees. They asked him, "Why then are you baptizing if you are neither the Messiah, nor Elijah, nor the prophet?" John answered them, "I baptize with water. Among you stands one whom you do not know, the one who is coming after me; I am not worthy to untie the thong of his sandal." This took place in Bethany across the Jordan where John was baptizing.

John 1:6–8, 19–28

*P*reparing for Christmas is my favorite activity as the days become short and the weather grows cold. I love getting ready for Christmas, and all that it entails: hanging the ornaments on the tree, spending extensive amounts of time choosing and wrapping Christmas gifts, and building gingerbread houses each year with my nieces. Summer is my favorite season, but when it comes to an end, I find solace through colder and shorter days that Christmas is on its way. I look forward to time spent during the season with family and friends. But these cherished traditions are preparations for the secular parts of the season. Even as a clergyperson whose profession is concerned with the spiritual, it takes time and effort to remind myself that we are not preparing just for the arrival of December 25; through the season of Advent, we are preparing for the coming of Christ in the past, present, and future. We are called to be active participants in living out God's kin-dom on earth.

Preparation: Putting the Plan into Action

For nearly thirty years, I worked beside my maternal grandmother to make dressing on Thanksgiving Day. In some regions, this iconic Thanksgiving dish is also known as stuffing. During my childhood, Grandma taught me all the parts of the dressing that could be prepared in advance. The sage could be rubbed from its stalks on Monday. The biscuits and cornbread could be baked as early as Tuesday, and this is preferrable because the dressing is best if the breads are a little stale. On Wednesday, the onions and celery could be chopped, and the celery could be boiled—both could be stored in the fridge overnight. On Thanksgiving Day, we placed all our prepared items, plus the other ingredients, on the counter before we started combining things in the mixing bowl.

Grandma spent time teaching me that preparation is key in the kitchen. Professional chefs use the French phrase *mise en place* (pronounced me-zahn-plahs) to mean having ingredients measured, cut, peeled, and so on before cooking begins. This includes making sure all necessary tools and equipment, like mixing bowls, pans, and whisks, are set out and ready to be used. This allows the cooking process to be smooth and efficient, rather than having to rush back to the pantry multiple times to get ingredients. For the home cook, *mise en place* (which translates literally into "put in place") means having everything laid out on the counter before the actual cooking begins. Most chefs recommend this for home cooks. Even though Grandma never used the phrase *mise en place*, she was still teaching me to practice it. Preparation matters.

If you want to see a solid example of churches taking preparation seriously, you need look no further than vacation Bible school (VBS). The intensity and focused preparation that goes into a week of hosting children is unrivaled. While the mental planning for VBS may begin months in advance, the physical preparations of setting up spaces usually occur in a flurry of activity one week or less before children start to arrive. In preparing for VBS, I have seen fellowship halls transformed into tropical islands, classrooms adorned with underwater seascapes, education wings decorated like intergalactic spaceports, and full-size rafts inflated on the chancel in the sanctuary. One church went so far as to build a whale in the sanctuary during a week of learning about Jonah.

Adults dress in all manner of costumes to both promote and teach at VBS. I have worn many such costumes myself; I have dressed as a scuba diver, a safari guide, an alien, and I have preached with a grass skirt tied over my clothing. My favorite costume of all time was the full-body dragon costume, although the large tail did keep me from being able to sit down properly. (After all, the apostle Paul did encourage us to be fools for Christ.)

Time is spent preparing the music the children will sing, printing lesson plans, reviewing instructions for games and activities, and preparing all the supplies for craft projects that will accompany the lesson. Preparations are made for themed snacks that tie in with each day's lesson, and sometimes lunch or dinner is provided each day for all the kids and volunteers.

Why do churches spend so much time preparing before VBS? There is something magical about transforming an ordinary space—ceiling tiles, fluorescent lights, neutral walls—into something spectacular. The organizers for the week hope to make the church an accessible space to kids with less formality and more bright colors. Choosing fun music and planning games are ways to get the kids excited about the week. But it goes far beyond the temporal; we put so much time into preparing for children to arrive because we want them to join us on a spiritual journey. The organizers hope to create a community in which the kids can have fun and feel safe while learning about the gospel. The preparation sets the stage for encounters with the Divine.

Never Been Home

In this week's passage, God has prepared the prophet Isaiah to proclaim that a new day has arrived for the Jewish people. Isaiah speaks of God's preparations for restorative justice and people's participation with grace in this new era. Most scholars say that this week's passage from Isaiah was written after the fall of the Babylonian Empire, meaning Isaiah 61 is offering words of hope to the Jewish people who have been allowed to leave their exile in Babylon and return to Judah.

In modern translations, the book of Isaiah changes from straightforward narrative in chapter 39 to elaborate poetry in chapter 40, meaning we can see a stylistic shift in the book. Additionally, Hebrew scholars confirm there is a drastic shift in language between the two chapters. The dramatic differences in the ancient Hebrew indicate that the two chapters were written at different points in history. Language changes over time; imagine reading a few lines of a Shakespearean sonnet juxtaposed with lyrics from Lin-Manuel Miranda. The difference is similar to the stark change in language happening in the book of Isaiah between chapters 39 and 40, leading scholars to believe that the book of Isaiah in our canon is a compilation of three books: the so-called First Isaiah (chapters 1–39) was written prior to Judah's defeat, Second Isaiah (chapters 40–55) was written during Babylonian captivity, and Third Isaiah (chapters 56–65) was written after the exile.

Upon first glance, it might seem like "going home" is not an occasion that should require a spiritual pep talk; it ought to have been a joyous occasion for the people of Judah. But on further reflection, consider that the people's exile in Babylon had extended for decades. The most conservative estimates of the length of the Jewish exile are around forty-eight years (and many say seventy years). Given that the average lifespan of people before modern medicine was about thirty-five years, by the end of the exile, very few people had memories of Judah as "home."

Consider it this way. I have a few ancestors from Scotland in my family tree. If someone walked up to me tomorrow and said, "Great news! You're going home!" and handed me a ticket to Glasgow, I would not be happy. I have nothing against Scotland—it's on my bucket list of places to visit—but it is certainly not my home. I would be a stranger in a foreign land.

Furthermore, the Jewish people are not returning to the wonderful homeland preserved in their parents' and grandparents' stories and memories. Instead, they are returning to a land that was devastated by the conquering Babylonians and then never rebuilt. In other books, such as Nehemiah, it is clear that the people returning from exile return not to Judah glorious but instead to Judah broken and devastated. The walls of Jerusalem have been torn down and never repaired. Beyond the shock of physical environment, they also face the realities of human nature, as it seems unlikely that the remnant of people who remained in Judah were eager to welcome their long-exiled neighbors. Strife and resentment seem likely as the exiled return and attempt to incorporate themselves into the remnant's community.

With all the complexities at play, this was a dire moment for the children of Abraham. They could choose to reunite and join forces or fall apart and drift away. The need for hope was high, and Isaiah offers the hope needed to prepare them for this difficult work of reuniting and living together.

In verse 1, we read, "The spirit of the Lord GOD is upon me, because the LORD has anointed me; he has sent me to bring good news to the oppressed, to bind up the brokenhearted, to proclaim liberty to the captives, and release to the prisoners." While a Christian view of this text might tend toward eisegesis of the word "spirit" ("eisegesis" means bringing to the text our Christian understandings and biases, in this case about the Holy Spirit), it is important to remember that Jewish people do not have a Trinitarian perspective on this text. Rather, the word "spirit" is translated from the Hebrew *ruach,* meaning spirit, wind, or breath.

Specific words within a culture can evoke specific images, memories, or even stories. If I ask an American-born English speaker what the letters E-I-E-I-O refer to, they might start humming the tune to "Old MacDonald Had a Farm." Outside the context of that culture, the letters would look like just that, a random collection of letters. But within the culture, those letters draw on something that is considered common knowledge. In the same way, the very mention of *ruach*—to the ears of ancient listeners—would immediately invoke the creation story in Genesis. Within the creation story, the *ruach* is the force behind the creation of all things. Indeed, in both Genesis and Ezekiel 37, we see examples of human beings with physical form who do not become fully alive until receiving God's *ruach*—the breath of life.

Invoking such imagery among the original audience in Isaiah indicates that the prophecy concerns creation or, in the case of Judah, re-creation. The God who ordered the cosmos out of chaos, the God who created all living things, is also powerful enough to bring restoration and hope to the people of Judah after their nation has been destroyed and Judah's people cast into exile in Babylon. The *ruach* of God will create a new thing.

This prophecy from Isaiah is preparing the people for the coming promise of a new day—when God will set right the wrongs that have been done. It is a call to prepare for the coming of God's justice to humankind. It is a call to prepare for the way of God, which will be different from the ways of humankind.

Who John Isn't

As we move from the text of Isaiah to this week's passage from the Gospel of John, we continue to see the theme of preparing through the life of John the Baptist. The Gospel of John tells the story of Jesus very differently than the other Gospels.

An icebreaker game common in youth groups is Two Truths and a Lie. In the game, individuals tell two truths and one lie about themselves, challenging the rest of the group to figure out which two statements are true and which is the lie. One of the reasons this game is fun is that it is counter to our normal social patterns. In the vast majority of social and professional settings, when people meet for the first time, they begin by sharing a few basic truths: their name, where they're from, and so on. Typically, we begin introductions with what we are, rather than what we are not.

The writer of the Fourth Gospel does not lie in his introduction of John the Baptist. But instead of beginning by telling the reader,

"Here is a short biography of who John is," he begins by telling the reader extensively who John is not. John is not the savior sent into the world, he is not Elijah or a prophet, and John is not the light. He is simply the messenger who has been sent to point to the light—to prepare the way for the coming of the light.

Although this passage spends so much time on who John is not, it also makes the purpose of John the Baptist incredibly clear: he has been sent to prepare the way for Jesus Christ. John is quoting Isaiah 40:3, in which the Babylonian exiles are advised to make a road to Jerusalem because God is promising the people in exile that they will one day return home. John refers to himself as the one who has been sent to "make straight the way of the Lord." Essentially, he is saying that he has been sent to prepare the world for its salvation.

After the writer has established who John is not, and then a little of who John is, we see John active in his ministry of baptizing believers in the Jordan River. But the question quickly becomes, Where does he get the idea to begin baptizing people? John the Baptist practices Judaism, so it is a safe bet to assume that his followers considered themselves Jewish as well. Many religions use water in cleansing rituals and holy ceremonies, including the religions that would have influenced John: Greek and Roman practices, as well as the Jewish tradition. There are some requirements for ritual cleansing in the Hebrew Scriptures, but baptism as it is practiced by John seems to be a practice that arose in the centuries between the youngest book of the Hebrew text and the birth of Jesus. A few Jewish sects were practicing baptism as a ritual at the time of John's ministry, so it is likely that John was a follower of one of these sects. Although the act—if not the theology—of baptism is commonly understood in modern Western culture, this would not have been true in John's time.

If we consider modern Christianity's understanding of baptism, it is in itself an act of preparation. "By Water and the Spirit" is a document created by The United Methodist Church that provides insight into the denomination's understanding of baptism. It states, "Baptism involves dying to sin, newness of life, union with Christ, receiving the Holy Spirit, and incorporation into Christ's church."[5] Thus the sacrament of baptism is an act of preparation, both for this life and for the life to come. The act of baptism incorporates all

Christians into the ongoing preparation of God's kin-dom on earth and the eternal kin-dom yet to come.

It's Beginning to Look a Lot like Christmas

When we are preparing our hearts, minds, and souls for the coming of Christ, what does that preparation look like? It will look a little different for each person, as God's call on your life is unique to you. If preparation in both domestic and holy realms is done through action, what actions will we take? Within the United Methodist liturgy for baptism or joining the church, all candidates are asked, "Do you accept the power that God gives you to resist evil, injustice, and oppression in whatever forms they present themselves?" While the language may be different, most Christian traditions have something similar within their baptismal covenants.

Part of preparing for the coming of Christ is to ask, "What can I do to resist evil, injustice, and oppression in whatever forms they present themselves?" And then put the answer to that question into action. Whether it is assisting people who need food and shelter through mercy ministries, working with local school programs to promote healthy and educated young people, or volunteering with agencies to combat justice issues that abound in our world (racism, sexism, classism, etc.), the work is plentiful, but the workers are few.

Preparing for the coming of Christ is taking an active role in the inbreaking of God's reign into this world, and this preparation is both-and work. We are called to do the spiritual work of preparing for Christ in our hearts and souls while also doing the hard work of enacting God's peace, justice, and mercy in the world. If I plan the perfect dinner party but leave all the ingredients in the refrigerator, my guests are not going to leave content. Hospitality requires preparation in both the physical and spiritual realms.

QUESTIONS FOR REFLECTION AND DISCUSSION

1. If you are using this book as a group study, consider beginning your session this week by playing Two Truths and a Lie. If you

are using this book as an individual, consider what two truths and a lie you would tell in a group. Keep in mind, the entire goal of the game is deception—you want everyone to guess that one of your truths is the lie!

2. The practice of *mise en place*—"put in place"—is used by chefs to make them more efficient. In the kitchen, it eases life to have all ingredients and tools prepared and handy before the cooking process begins. Are there other parts of life where this holds true? How might this practice apply in your work? hobbies? general life?

3. Recall a time when you have been a part of an event or activity that required extensive preparation. What was it like? What did the prep work entail? How long did preparations take?

4. Consider a time when you were completely prepared for an unexpected event. Perhaps you were at work, on a trip, or even at home. What did it mean that you were prepared when the unexpected took place? What tools (physical or mental) did you have in place in advance?

5. The Jewish people returning from exile were likely unprepared for the reality of arriving "home." Describe a time when you felt unprepared for events in your life. Was there any way to be prepared? How might God have worked through that experience to prepare a new way in your journey?

6. How might baptism be perceived as a type of preparation? What is the significance of baptism in your tradition?

7. As the secular preparations for Christmas continue to amplify in the coming days, how can you continue to keep your soul focused on the anticipatory meaning of Advent? How are you preparing for the spiritual part of Christmas, the coming of Jesus Christ?

Find the companion video for week three of Advent at http://tiny.cc /StayAwhileSession3.

DAILY REFLECTIONS

Monday

When I was in college, my campus ministry hosted a white elephant gift exchange every year. The gifts were supposed to be funny or clever and cost no more than five dollars. There were many complicated rules to this gift exchange, including the ability to steal another person's gift or choose a different one for yourself. However, no one was allowed to unwrap their gift until the very end of the event. The most elaborately wrapped packages might not contain the best presents.

The second year I participated in this event, knowing the rules in advance, I purchased the special white chocolate-dipped Oreos that are available only in winter. This is one of two major exceptions to my preference for homemade Christmas-season indulgences. (I will write about the other one in another day's devotional.) I then proceeded to do an extremely poor job of wrapping the box of cookies in old newspaper.

My gift was the last one chosen at the gift exchange. I laughed to myself as no one picked my present and laughed again as the last person looked crestfallen to be "stuck" with my gift, the only present remaining. I kept an eye on the person opening my present when it came time to unwrap the gifts. Sure enough, they suddenly were excited when they realized they had gotten a delicious gift wrapped in lousy packaging. I don't remember what beautifully wrapped white elephant gift I received that year—but I do remember it was either ugly or cheesy, not something I kept or enjoyed.

Have there been times you have been prepared for the worst, and then something delightful has taken place? When have you been delightfully surprised by God, or delightfully surprised by other people? Have you ever received a delightful surprise that came in ugly packaging? What do these experiences teach us about our secular lives and our spiritual lives?

Tuesday

What are you doing to prepare for Christmas? Buying and wrapping gifts? Decorating your home with a tree and Christmas lights? Planning to get together with family and friends? How are you also preparing for the coming of Christ in the past, present, and future? Take a few moments today to write down some notes about how you can prepare, acting with your heart, mind, and soul, for the coming of Christ.

Wednesday

When my nieces were very young, I began the tradition of making gingerbread houses with them every year during the Christmas season. We schedule a night when the girls spend the night at our house and then celebrate Christmas with my husband's father the following morning. On the night before our celebration, we build our gingerbread houses. The next morning, we decorate them with candy. I often prepare gingerbread for the houses from scratch a few weeks before Christmas. This allows the gingerbread time to dry before we use it as a building material, and it has the added bonus of filling the house with the most beautiful aroma of ginger throughout the holiday season.

The girls are both teenagers now but consider this a part of how our family celebrates Christmas. What are the traditions you are preparing to carry out this Christmas season? Why are they important to you or your family? Do these traditions intersect with your spiritual life? If so, in what ways? If they do not, how might they this year?

Thursday

My paternal grandmother was known for making certain that no one ever left her house hungry—and her baking skills assured that no one would ever choose to do so. By the time my sister and I came along, my grandfather had retired, and Grandma no longer had tables of farmhands to feed on a regular basis. Nonetheless, she continued pouring her energy into her culinary efforts.

In preparation for her funeral, the presiding pastor asked my immediate family, "What was the best thing she made?" He immediately got three different responses from the four of us. Dad said it was her cinnamon rolls, my sister said it was her chocolate cake, and I insisted it was her cherry pie. During her life, to accommodate these different preferences, Grandma would prepare for our visits by making three desserts in advance—assuring that we would each have our favorite.

Consider a time a person has done a great deal of preparation for an encounter with you. What were the circumstances? How did it make you feel? How might such an encounter demonstrate for us all the extravagance of God's love?

Friday

While I was in college, an adult named Lynlee volunteered with the campus ministry I attended. In the years I was in school, Lynlee frequently opened up her home for the students from the ministry to gather for movie nights. She kept a large Tupperware tub in her kitchen, and she prepared for these movie nights by consistently keeping it well stocked with plenty of excellent movie night snacks.

Lynlee's generosity and hospitality set an excellent example for me later in life, when I became a campus minister myself and frequently welcomed students from the ministry into my home. She was well prepared for students coming into her home, and it was marvelous to be welcomed into a real home when we were still living in student housing and apartments.

Who in your own life has demonstrated generous and excellent hospitality? Who has welcomed you when you needed to be welcomed? How can these encounters be examples of God's prevenient grace, the grace that goes before us?

Saturday

In the 1980s, advertisers developed a slogan for Motel 6 that was used for years: "We'll leave the light on for you." Who among us doesn't appreciate when a member of our household thinks of our late arrival and leaves a light on? This slogan combines the sentiments "We'll welcome you as if you're coming home" and "We are prepared for your arrival." As a guest, what signals to you that you are welcome and that your host is ready for you to arrive? God didn't wait until humanity was ready for the arrival of Jesus, and Jesus came anyway. What might be signs in our households and communities that we are ready for the arrival of Jesus in the past, present, and future?

Fourth Sunday of Advent

WELCOME

Zephaniah 3:14–20; Luke 1:39–55

Sing aloud, O daughter Zion;
   shout, O Israel!
Rejoice and exult with all your heart,
   O daughter Jerusalem!
The LORD has taken away the judgments against you,
   he has turned away your enemies.
The king of Israel, the LORD, is in your midst;
   you shall fear disaster no more.
On that day it shall be said to Jerusalem:
Do not fear, O Zion;
   do not let your hands grow weak.
The LORD, your God, is in your midst,
   a warrior who gives victory;
he will rejoice over you with gladness,
   he will renew you in his love;
he will exult over you with loud singing
   as on a day of festival.
I will remove disaster from you,
   so that you will not bear reproach for it.
I will deal with all your oppressors
   at that time.
And I will save the lame
   and gather the outcast,
and I will change their shame into praise
   and renown in all the earth.
At that time I will bring you home,
   at the time when I gather you;

for I will make you renowned and praised
    among all the peoples of the earth,
when I restore your fortunes
    before your eyes, says the LORD.

Zephaniah 3:14–20

In those days Mary set out and went with haste to a Judean
town in the hill country, where she entered the house of
Zechariah and greeted Elizabeth. When Elizabeth heard
Mary's greeting, the child leaped in her womb. And Elizabeth was filled with the Holy Spirit and exclaimed with a
loud cry, "Blessed are you among women, and blessed is the
fruit of your womb. And why has this happened to me, that
the mother of my Lord comes to me? For as soon as I heard
the sound of your greeting, the child in my womb leaped for
joy. And blessed is she who believed that there would be a
fulfillment of what was spoken to her by the Lord."
    And Mary said,

"My soul magnifies the Lord,
    and my spirit rejoices in God my Savior,
for he has looked with favor on the lowliness of his
        servant.
    Surely, from now on all generations will call me
        blessed;
for the Mighty One has done great things for me,
    and holy is his name.
His mercy is for those who fear him
    from generation to generation.
He has shown strength with his arm;
    he has scattered the proud in the thoughts of their
        hearts.
He has brought down the powerful from their thrones,
    and lifted up the lowly;
he has filled the hungry with good things,
    and sent the rich away empty.
He has helped his servant Israel,
    in remembrance of his mercy,
according to the promise he made to our ancestors,
    to Abraham and to his descendants forever."

Luke 1:39–55

*O*ne Christmas Eve, I noticed two young women come into the sanctuary just as worship was beginning. In small communities, it is easy to know everyone, or at least know how they are related to the people I do know; in most churches, visitors with no connections have a nervous look that tends to be recognizable. I immediately recognized by their body language that these two young women were visitors. When worship was over, I made my way over to introduce myself and asked if they were from the area. One woman began, "I grew up here, but now my partner and I live on the East Coast. We came home to spend the holidays with my family. Everyone went to church this evening, but we knew we wouldn't be welcome at my childhood church. I had heard around town that we might be welcome here."

I responded, "You are always welcome here! I hope you come back the next time you visit, and I hope other folks made that clear!" They assured me that nearly everyone had spoken to them and encouraged them to come to worship the next time they were in town.

We all long for the acceptance of a warm welcome. At out-of-town conferences, surrounded by clergy, I've paused for a few moments holding my lunch, nervous about where to sit. Logically, I know this is ridiculous. I've yet to approach a table of colleagues who responded, "No. You can't sit here." But from the small child in the cafeteria holding a lunch tray all the way to the new resident at the retirement home holding a similar tray, we never outgrow that nagging question: "Where will I be welcome?"

As we prepare to welcome the coming Christ this Christmas, we look to how God has welcomed us into the kin-dom, and therefore how we might extend that welcome to others.

A Taste of Home

My mother, a high school teacher, gave birth to me during her school's summer break. When school began in the fall, she went back to her full-time work of teaching and coaching. My parents had a family friend babysit me, and Judy was one of my primary caregivers through the first few years of my life. One evening when I was a teenager, I was greeted by the most glorious smell as I entered the kitchen, and I asked my mom what she was cooking. "It's Cajun rice, a recipe Judy used to make all the time."

The moment I took my first bite of the dish, I was struck with overwhelming nostalgia. I had been craving the dish for years but hadn't remembered what it was. Although I could not call it up in active memory, I had eaten it frequently during those early years at Judy's house, and the smell and taste took me back to that space in which I was safe and well loved; eating the dish felt like being welcomed home.

In the English language, "welcome" can be used as a verb, adjective, interjection, or noun, which means that there is wide variety in how we use this single word. For our purposes, we will explore two aspects of welcome. The first is the actual threshold moment when company arrives at the door—what action do we take to welcome guests into our homes as host, and what actions make us feel welcome when we arrive as a guest? The second is the sensation of welcomeness—where do we feel welcome, and what gives us that impression?

Both types of welcome are intimately connected; sometimes we feel so welcome in other people's homes that we do not expect a threshold welcome at all. When I arrive at my Aunt Freda's home for holiday celebrations, I let myself in the front door with a shouted "Hello!" and immediately begin helping in the kitchen. I do not expect anyone to offer to take my coat or get me a drink—I understand that I am welcome in such a deep way that I am more than comfortable making myself at home. On the other side, if I am welcoming someone who has never been to my house before, creating a warm welcome necessitates that I greet them, show them around, and ask if I can get them anything. Feelings of familiarity and welcomeness negate any need for a formal welcome in some situations, but the lack of familiarity necessitates such a welcome for newcomers in others.

Durng my first year of college, I was so homesick that I frequently cried myself to sleep at night. I remember bursting into tears the first time I went home, because—even though it was only for the weekend—I was so happy to finally be home again. It wasn't just the familiarity, but the warmth and welcome home provides. Before I'd left home, I'd grown irritated that my parents needed to know my minute-to-minute itinerary whenever I left the house, but after leaving, I found sorrow in having no one who cared what time I arrived back in my residence hall. Walking into my dorm room sometimes garnered a grunted "Hey" from my roommate—hardly a warm or enthusiastic welcome. Walking through the door of my childhood home meant warm hugs from my parents, my sister, and my best friend, and exuberant tail wags from our dog.

Welcomed Home

The prophet Zephaniah was likely unaccustomed to warm welcomes, because much of his prophecy contained damning news for his audience. Zephaniah's ministry is placed in the time period after the fall of Israel to the Assyrians but before the fall of Judah to the Babylonians. Most likely, he prophesied in Jerusalem at the beginning of King Josiah's reform movement. However, Josiah's reforms ended with his untimely death (609 BCE), and Jerusalem fell to the Babylonians in 597 BCE.

The first two chapters of Zephaniah contain horrific warnings of what will happen to Judah if they do not reform their ways, repent of their sins, and turn back toward God. These first two chapters contain intimidating phrases, such as God saying, "I will cut off humanity from the face of the earth. . . . I will stretch out my hand against Judah, and against all the inhabitants of Jerusalem" (1:3b–4a). The first chapter of Zephaniah highlights how the people of Judah have become unfaithful to Yahweh and have begun to worship the god Baal. In chapter 2, Zephaniah's prophecy condemns the other nations of the world.

In chapter 3, Zephaniah suddenly turns to words of assurance and the promise of rescue, even though the previous two chapters of the book have highlighted that humankind is to blame for their own constant need of rescue. The final verse of chapter 3 is one with which all humans can resonate: "At that time I will bring you home, at the time when I gather you." Who does not want to be welcomed home?

For those of us who have been fortunate enough to have a place to call home where we have felt safe and loved, there are few things better than a genuine homecoming welcome at the end of a journey or time spent away. Because this homecoming is likely a prophetic reference to the end of Judah's eventual exile, the welcome that goes hand in hand with the joys of coming home cannot be downplayed or overestimated.

Welcoming the Divine

While most of Zephaniah's prophecies likely meant he was rarely greeted with a warm welcome from his peers, in this week's New Testament passage, Mary is welcomed with joy and excitement by her cousin Elizabeth. Luke 1:46–55 is often referred to as the Magnificat, taken from the Latin word for "magnify" in verse 46. When we explore Scripture, historical context is important for understanding the text. While the Magnificat may be viewed at first glance as a beautiful song of praise to God, it is particularly important to understand Mary's cultural status to fully appreciate the subversive nature of this passage. Mary is Jewish, and the Jewish people are living under Roman occupation. While Israel was under Roman occupation, the vast majority of Jewish persons did not have the rights and privileges that accompanied Roman citizenship. Furthermore, Mary is a woman surrounded by both the patriarchal culture of her Jewish heritage and the patriarchal nature of the Roman Empire; everywhere she turns, men are the ones with power. To add to Mary's lowly status at that time and place in history, she is also most likely a teenager, because in her context, most fathers arranged to marry off their daughters while the girls were still in their teenage years. Culturally, if a community even suspected a girl was no longer a virgin before marriage, she essentially became unmarriageable, bringing shame on herself and her family. Marrying girls shortly after they began menstruating helped keep potential scandals at bay.

To summarize: Mary is an unwed pregnant teenager in a strictly patriarchal society, living in a country where her people are under occupation of a foreign military. I don't know about you, but if I were choosing the circumstances under which God incarnate would enter the world, this would not be my first choice; this is the opposite of a warm welcome.

And yet this is how God chose to enter the world, and the unlikely nature of this choice is exemplified in the subversive nature of Mary's song, and John welcoming Jesus, even from within Elizabeth's womb. Mary claims women's power as the bringers of life, insisting that despite her lowly circumstances, "all generations will call me blessed." Mary claims that God will assure the proud and powerful are overturned—a proclamation bordering on treason for someone living under foreign military occupation. She sings that the hungry will be filled with good things and the rich will be sent away empty— a complete overhaul of the values upheld by most societies, even into our own time. This is a precursor to Jesus' Beatitudes, declarations that turn humanity's expectations of power and wealth on their heads. Mary makes clear that the kin-dom of God welcomes all of God's children, especially those whom our world might frequently classify as unwelcome.

The Magnificat, Mary's song, welcomes the inbreaking of God's reign on earth. Her song reflects the well-known words from the Lord's Prayer, "Thy kingdom come, thy will be done, on earth as it is in heaven." She is welcoming God's presence entering into the world.

Safe and Wanted

As Mary's song welcomes God into the world, how do we think of welcoming other people? What are the keys to feeling welcome? I believe there are two primary elements of feeling welcome: (1) feeling safe and (2) feeling wanted. If the first element of that equation, "safe," feels strange to you, it is likely you lead a life with a reasonable amount of privilege. Many people regularly enter situations in which they feel they might be in danger from others based on elements beyond their control. Unfortunately, our churches have been historically unsafe places for a myriad of people. Feeling unsafe, or in danger, can often be a result of race, gender, sexual orientation, language, gender identity, nationality, immigration status, and many other factors.

But beyond physical safety, there is also the sense of safety in terms of psychological and social safety. To feel truly welcome, we must feel as if we can be ourselves—that we will not be rejected for revealing the truths about who we are. In other words, is it safe to be me? Can I be authentic in this setting? In a lot of situations, the answer to that question is a resounding no. Most of us, including me, use strong filters when we are out in the world where we do not know the opinions or biases of the people we meet. But when we know we are safely in the presence of people who deeply love us—who will not reject us if we speak the whole truth—we are more apt to do so.

During the time I served as a campus minister, a group of college students in the ministry came together and expressed a desire to reclaim our connection to Reconciling Ministries, the organization that supports the full inclusion of LGBTQ persons in The United Methodist Church. At the time, I believed these students might be concerned for their friends or other students who might be drawn to the ministry. I knew the students well, and all of them had been in at least one heterosexual relationship and presented as cisgender. I happily reclaimed our status as a Reconciling Ministry with the support of the ministry's board and didn't give it much additional thought.

However, over the years, many of the students (not all, but a decent number) who were most passionate about us being a Reconciling Ministry have come out of the closet as LGBTQ. As I watched one student after another come out of the closet in later years, I began to realize that they weren't asking, "Will my friends be welcome here?" They were *really* asking, "If I tell you who I am, will I be welcome here?" While I think the first question is important, the second question began to make me ponder what it meant to be assured that they would still be welcome after they figured out some important pieces of their identities. Being assured that they would be welcome gave them a safe place to continue their spiritual journeys.

Welcome and Comfortable Aren't Synonyms

While I defined feeling welcome as feeling safe and wanted, as I pondered the meaning of welcome, I removed what had originally been a third part of my definition: feeling comfortable. Being welcome does not always mean that a person feels comfortable or unchallenged. When I am welcomed into a culture that is different from my own, it may be the warmest and most culturally appropriate welcome in the world—but if it is different from what I am accustomed to, I may experience some discomfort.

When my husband was on a mission trip in rural Kenya, the community hosting him slaughtered a goat and roasted it whole on a spit. A friend informed him that this was a huge honor in the village. Watching the whole goat turn all day on the spit (not a regular sight in our part of the midwestern United States) made him slightly squeamish, but he understood the importance of showing appreciation for this act of hospitality and sacrifice by the hosts. He was being welcomed with abundance. While he was not entirely comfortable, the intent of their welcoming gesture was unmistakable.

Sometimes providing hospitality can also stretch our realms of comfort. A friend of mine hosted a large family gathering in her home not long after a family member had come out as transgender. While my friend greeted this announcement with welcome, not everyone in her family felt the same, and she knew the gathering might be a challenge. Despite her best attempts, some people in the family were not pleased with the welcome she extended and were frustrated and even angered by her use of the family member's new name and preferred pronouns. Although she felt she did the right thing, the gathering was made uncomfortable by those who did not welcome the transition.

I also removed "comfortable" from the definition because in spaces of faith, there are a multitude of times we ought to be uncomfortable. How can we possibly grow or change if we always feel comfortable? If we are never challenged? I should be uncomfortable about my own white privilege and the injustice of racism. I should be uncomfortable about my economic privilege when children are going to bed hungry at night. I should be uncomfortable about the privilege of my nationality when immigrant children in my country are being kept in cages. Being a person of faith means we are often going to be led to places of growth, and growth is frequently motivated by discomfort.

No transformation can take place without change. But it is possible to be both welcome and uncomfortable at the same time. As an English-speaking American (a position of privilege), I am very accustomed to my language being the lingua franca. However, I've been at dinners where I didn't speak or understand the primary language being spoken around the table. Although I have found these experiences a little uncomfortable—I couldn't understand most of the dinner conversations—this did not lessen the undeniable hospitality of my hosts. I was still greeted with smiles and enthusiastically offered more food when my plate was empty, and usually someone at the table could interpret the best jokes into English for me. Even in the midst of discomfort, we can still feel completely welcome; we can still feel fully safe and fully wanted.

Safe and wanted are both conveyed as part of a warm welcome in the texts from Zephaniah and Luke, but Mary's words in Luke best highlight what it might mean to be welcome (safe and wanted) but a little uncomfortable. God's overturn of the world's social order in Mary's prophecy is enough to cause discomfort for those of us in places of privilege. But, if we read this text closely, it also carries a promise and profoundly good news; Mary's welcome of God's kin-dom on earth contains the promise of God's mercy and goodness.

When we are welcomed into God's kin-dom, we are called upon to extend that same welcome to those who also want to participate. It is easy to extend welcome to those we already love, but Scripture commands us to welcome the stranger, the refugee, and the outcast. We are called to welcome our neighbors—in some cases, this may entail the first step of simply meeting our neighbors. While not every welcome can be filled with comfort on the part of the host or guest, it can be filled with the promise that an earthly welcome can be the first step toward a heavenly welcome in God's kin-dom.

Many of us experienced some level of exile during the early days of the COVID-19 pandemic. Despite all of technology's best advances, we learned repeatedly that there are no replacements for presence; there is no substitute for being together in community. As we learn to welcome those around us, we also learn to welcome the coming of Jesus through the season of Advent. May we throw open the doors and welcome God's people, creating homes, churches, and communities where all people can feel safe and wanted.

QUESTIONS FOR REFLECTION AND DISCUSSION

1. Tell the story of a time you felt unwelcome. What were the circumstances? Were people openly hostile, or were there passive-aggressive hints that you were not welcome? What was the experience like? How did you feel when you left this encounter?

2. Now share the story of a time you felt incredibly welcomed. How did you know you were welcome? What were some of the elements that made you feel welcome? What made you want to go back into that environment after such a positive experience?
3. What do you think about the notion that "comfortable" does not need to be a part of a welcoming environment? Have you ever had an experience in which you felt incredibly welcomed but also a little (or a lot!) uncomfortable? What were the circumstances, and how did you feel welcome despite some discomfort?
4. Have you ever felt some discomfort as the host of an event in trying to create hospitable space for all your guests? What was the situation, and what about it made you feel uncomfortable?
5. Zephaniah tends to be one of the lesser-known books of the Bible. What did you learn about Zephaniah in this chapter? How does this Scripture frame a long-awaited homecoming for God's people?
6. Mary's Song (the Magnificat) sometimes gets lost in the excitement of telling the Christmas story. How might Mary's words have been controversial in her time? How might they be controversial in our time? Who does Mary believe God will welcome into the kin-dom to come?
7. What steps can you take to welcome God's people? How can you help create homes, churches, and communities where all of God's children can feel safe and wanted?

Find the companion video for week four of Advent at http://tiny.cc/StayAwhileSession4.

DAILY REFLECTIONS

Monday

Not long ago, while in an unfamiliar part of my home city, I visited a local coffee shop. The coffee shop had a roaster for roasting coffee beans sitting near the front door, next to the front counter. While I waited for my order, I began watching the roaster at work. I could smell the delicious caramel aromas coming off the roasting beans as they spun around inside the machine. Noting my interest, a man came from behind the counter and, without me saying a word, launched into a long explanation of what was happening with the roaster and why he believed air-roasting coffee beans on-site created the best product possible. He explained variations in roasting temperatures, the importance of rapid cooling in the process, and other interesting points. This man was in love with producing excellent coffee. I was so inspired by his passion and enthusiasm, I simply had to go back to the cash register and order a bag of these freshly roasted coffee beans.

The punch line to this story? I don't drink coffee. My original order was a cup of tea. But I purchased a bag of coffee anyway. I figured I could give it to my husband to take to work or pass it along to a family member. This stranger's enthusiasm for his craft inspired me to action.

How can enthusiasm be an important part of a warm welcome? How might contagious excitement be shared when we welcome people into our homes, churches, and other aspects of our communities? How can this help build the kin-dom of God?

Tuesday

In my high school and middle school, there were rules on who was welcome at certain tables in the cafeteria. These rules were not written down or officially kept by any adult on the premises, but every student in the building knew the rules and played by them. When a person did not play by the rules, they were ostracized.

In middle school, we were allowed to have only six people per table. My group of friends sat at the same table at lunch every day. When someone who did not belong in our group of six tried to sit at our table, I am ashamed to say that we made it clear that person was not welcome. Don't get me wrong—I was very far from being in the popular crowd in my school days. But nonetheless, my group of friends still formed a tight-knit and exclusive clique.

In high school, the cafeteria had an inset floor with three levels. The first level down was where underclassmen sat during lunch, and the lowest level in the center was designated for upperclassmen. Once again, no teacher or adult ever informed us of these rules—they were not rules created or enforced by adults. But we all understood them just the same. Very few students were bold enough to dare to eat lunch in the center lower level until they were upperclassmen.

And this is what being unwelcome can look like. It might not even entail anything said out loud or conveyed on paper. It might simply be understood through body language, the angle of an eyebrow, the tilt of a chin.

When have unspoken cues made you feel unwelcome? What was the experience like? How can you use that experience to make others feel more welcome in similar circumstances? What can you do to assure that people feel welcome in your home and in your faith community? What does this teach us about the importance of all people feeling welcome in the kin-dom of God?

Wednesday

In my first appointment out of seminary, I served as the associate pastor at a large congregation. One family who regularly attended the 10:30 a.m. worship service had three girls, and the youngest was Liz. Though she was still in elementary school at the time, to this day, I believe Liz was the best church greeter I have ever witnessed. When visitors came to our service, she immediately befriended them and welcomed them to sit with her and her family. She would introduce me to visitors by saying, "These are my new friends _____," and calling them all by name. I usually asked new members who joined the church what kept them coming back after their initial visit—and on more than one occasion, people brought up Liz's name.

Fifteen years after our introduction, she is now an adult, and I have not been her pastor for a long time. These days, I am privileged to count Liz among my friends. Visiting a faith community as a stranger is an incredible act of courage, and Liz met this act with one of her own by providing a welcome worthy of the visitors' courage.

What would it look like if all faith communities had their own version of Liz? What would it look like to greet strangers in such a warm and welcoming way? How might this change the shape of our communities? How might this change the kin-dom of God?

Thursday

On the television show *Cheers,* everyone in the bar shouts out "Norm!" whenever Norman Peterson, played by George Wendt, walks into the bar. While I have never frequented any bar enough to garner this welcome, I have experienced it in church environments and in one local coffee shop. The feeling of being welcomed by name by a multitude of people is incredible and lights up my day.

How can we create these experiences for other people? Jesus is in the midst of telling a parable about a king when he says in Matthew 25:40, "Truly I tell you, just as you did it to one of the least of these who are members of my family, you did it to me." If this is true, in what practical ways might we be able to welcome Jesus as we continue to prepare for the coming of Christ?

Friday

No matter how warmly I dress, when I spend a great deal of time outside in very cold weather, there is no thought more welcoming than looking toward the moment I get to go indoors, enfold myself in a blanket, and wrap my hands around a cup of hot chocolate. If I have been outside after dark, the light is also an incredibly welcome change.

Consider what makes you feel welcome and cozy. Contemplate a scene that encompasses this feeling for you in your own life. What makes you feel welcome? What makes you feel at home? How might this translate into welcoming others? How might it translate into welcoming Jesus this Christmas?

Saturday

Even though we do not have a dog in our household, when it comes to cats versus dogs, I'm a dog person. Most cats possess a level of indifference that I find off-putting. Cat people, say what you will about me, but I'm not ashamed to admit that I need more devotion and attention than that. I know of no creature that can match the unbridled enthusiasm of a dog excited to welcome the people it knows. Sure, my goats and chickens come running when they see me—but it's because they expect snacks. Dogs will come happily running, tails wagging, even if they know with certainty that there are no snacks in their immediate future.

What can human beings learn from this sort of enthusiastic welcome? What can we learn about how God welcomes humankind from this sort of boundless joy in welcoming people home?

Christmas Eve

Stay Awhile

Isaiah 9:2–7; Luke 2:1–20; John 1:1–14

The people who walked in darkness
    have seen a great light;
those who lived in a land of deep darkness—
    on them light has shined.
You have multiplied the nation,
    you have increased its joy;
they rejoice before you
    as with joy at the harvest,
    as people exult when dividing plunder.
For the yoke of their burden,
    and the bar across their shoulders,
    the rod of their oppressor,
    you have broken as on the day of Midian.
For all the boots of the tramping warriors
    and all the garments rolled in blood
    shall be burned as fuel for the fire.
For a child has been born for us,
    a son given to us;
authority rests upon his shoulders;
    and he is named
Wonderful Counselor, Mighty God,
    Everlasting Father, Prince of Peace.
His authority shall grow continually,
    and there shall be endless peace
for the throne of David and his kingdom.
    He will establish and uphold it

67

with justice and with righteousness
from this time onward and forevermore.
The zeal of the LORD of hosts will do this.

Isaiah 9:2–7

In those days a decree went out from Emperor Augustus that all the world should be registered. This was the first registration and was taken while Quirinius was governor of Syria. All went to their own towns to be registered. Joseph also went from the town of Nazareth in Galilee to Judea, to the city of David called Bethlehem, because he was descended from the house and family of David. He went to be registered with Mary, to whom he was engaged and who was expecting a child. While they were there, the time came for her to deliver her child. And she gave birth to her firstborn son and wrapped him in bands of cloth, and laid him in a manger, because there was no place for them in the inn.

In that region there were shepherds living in the fields, keeping watch over their flock by night. Then an angel of the Lord stood before them, and the glory of the Lord shone around them, and they were terrified. But the angel said to them, "Do not be afraid; for see—I am bringing you good news of great joy for all the people: to you is born this day in the city of David a Savior, who is the Messiah, the Lord. This will be a sign for you: you will find a child wrapped in bands of cloth and lying in a manger." And suddenly there was with the angel a multitude of the heavenly host, praising God and saying,

"Glory to God in the highest heaven,
    and on earth peace among those whom he favors!"

When the angels had left them and gone into heaven, the shepherds said to one another, "Let us go now to Bethlehem and see this thing that has taken place, which the Lord has made known to us." So they went with haste and found Mary and Joseph, and the child lying in the manger. When they saw this, they made known what had been told them about this child; and all who heard it were amazed at what the shepherds told them. But Mary treasured all these words and pondered them in her heart. The shepherds returned, glorifying and praising God for all they had heard and seen, as it had been told them.

Luke 2:1–20

In the beginning was the Word, and the Word was with God, and the Word was God. He was in the beginning with God. All things came into being through him, and without him not one thing came into being. What has come into being in him was life, and the life was the light of all people. The light shines in the darkness, and the darkness did not overcome it.

There was a man sent from God, whose name was John. He came as a witness to testify to the light, so that all might believe through him. He himself was not the light, but he came to testify to the light. The true light, which enlightens everyone, was coming into the world.

He was in the world, and the world came into being through him; yet the world did not know him. He came to what was his own, and his own people did not accept him. But to all who received him, who believed in his name, he gave power to become children of God, who were born, not of blood or of the will of the flesh or of the will of man, but of God.

And the Word became flesh and lived among us, and we have seen his glory, the glory as of a father's only son, full of grace and truth.

John 1:1–14

*I*n the days leading up to Christmas, many parts of our society become a flurry of activity. People crowd airports and highways in frantic attempts to live into the song "I'll Be Home for Christmas." Any place with commerce begins to buzz as people make last-minute gift and food purchases in preparation for Christmas Day. Children spend these days school-free and awaiting the big day with a hyper anticipation reserved for youth. Those who are hosting celebrations spend endless hours in kitchens, chopping, simmering, stirring, and baking. Presents are wrapped and placed under the tree.

A great deal of effort goes into the secular parts of Christmas in many American families, and there can be a feeling of letdown when the dinner and the gift exchange are over. I'm no Grinch; I thoroughly enjoy the secular trappings of Christmas, too. But there is a moment I look forward to, when the main meal has been eaten, presents have been unwrapped, and we sit around and enjoy spending time with one another. We simply want to stay awhile in one another's presence.

God loves us so very much that God wanted to be present with us. And while the physical person of Jesus stayed only a very little while, the promise that came with Jesus' life, teaching, death, and resurrection is a promise that has true staying power. God is with us, and not just at Christmas.

Stay Awhile

During seminary, very few of my friends lived close enough to travel to their homes for occasions like Easter. Since most of us also served as interns in churches near our seminary, we were expected to work during Holy Week and Easter morning. So we had a tradition of getting together on the evening of Easter Sunday for a "family dinner." My friend Todd usually prepared the main dish in a spectacular fashion, and the rest of us brought side dishes for a potluck. We all lived in apartments or shared a house with roommates, so when our entire friend group gathered into one space, it was a tight squeeze. But, as most of us were in our early twenties, we were perfectly content to find an open spot on the floor or sofa when it came time to eat our Easter dinner—none of us had a table or space that would accommodate us all.

Even though these gatherings were far from formal, they hold a special place in my memory. We were all entirely exhausted from the stresses of Holy Week in our churches and the ordinary weight of our course loads. But, once the work of helping others celebrate the risen Christ was complete, we found time to enjoy our own celebration. One Easter, after we had eaten, we began discussing how much schoolwork we still had waiting for us before we would be able to call it a night. One of my wise friends spoke up and reminded us all, "Christ is risen today; the rest is just stuff. Sit back and enjoy."

In other words: stay awhile. The best part of hosting isn't inviting, planning, preparing, or welcoming. The best part of a celebratory gathering is toward the end, when everyone is full, laughing, telling stories. It isn't the frantic rushing around the kitchen—it is sitting down with guests and the immense joy of good company.

When I served as a pastor in campus ministry, our organization did not have a building of its own, so my husband and I hosted most activities in our home. On more than one occasion, I tried to move Bible studies onto campus, thinking this would be more convenient for the students (and my spouse). But repeatedly, the students unanimously requested to meet at my house again—even though it meant trekking out to their cars, asking one another for rides, and driving a few miles away from campus.

For a long time, I did not understand why they wanted events to be held at our house. I was bringing the same quality snacks to on-campus events. I was using the same curriculum we had been doing in my home. I reached out to some of my former students to ask them the question directly: "Why did you want to continue meeting at my house?"

Initially, I received a few of the more flippant answers I expected. "Your couch was comfortable" and "You had great blankets for us to wrap up in." One former student, now a colleague, responded, "You made us better snacks at your house!"

But then the answers began to go deeper. The students loved being in a real home. At the time, my husband and I lived in a small, three-bedroom ranch house. Sometimes we had to squeeze into the tight quarters of our living room, but the students loved being someplace they all felt at home—someplace where they were welcome, safe, and secure. Someplace they knew they were loved and valued. They needed a space where they could be authentically themselves and would never be turned away. They wanted to feel at home. Simply put, they wanted someplace to stay awhile.

Come In out of the Cold

We see this deep human need for a safe place to call home in this week's Isaiah text. This passage is part of First Isaiah, the collection of writings composed after the northern kingdom, Israel, has fallen to the Assyrians but before the southern kingdom, Judah, fell to the Babylonians.

In Isaiah 9, Isaiah is speaking to the people of Judah, who are living in a new level of fear—if Israel could fail, Judah might be next.

They had not imagined that Yahweh would allow their nations to fail. The nation of Judah was also under immense strain from the Assyrian government, whose armies consistently attempted to expand the boundaries of the Assyrian Empire, therefore putting pressure on the stretched resources of Judah.

The prophet's emphasis on peace throughout this passage is no surprise given the historical context. The people of Judah lived in a constant state of fear and foreboding. Isaiah's assurance to them is that someday there will be rest from the violence and danger—someday there will be peace. Isaiah is giving them a day to look forward to because in their present situation, hope is hard to come by. Isaiah's declaration of future peace goes so far as to proclaim that on that day, even the tools of war—boots and bloodstained garments—will be destroyed, because they will no longer be needed.

Isaiah writes, "The people who walked in darkness have seen a great light; those who lived in a land of deep darkness—on them light has shined." In other words, Isaiah is promising them that one day, those who have wandered in the night will come back to hearth and home.

That is fundamentally what hospitality is, creating a space in which people feel safe and unconditionally loved. Isaiah promises them: one day, you will come in from the dark and cold, sit beside the fire, relish the warmth and light, and sip from a warm cup. The people are in need of comfort, and they are in need of assurance that this darkness will not last forever. One day, they will live in the light again; one day, they will feel at home again.

Presence Matters

Moving into the Gospel of Luke, the story of the first Christmas takes place far from the Holy Family's home. A common challenge for many pastors preaching Luke's Gospel at Christmas is many parishioners' perceived familiarity with the story. People *think* they already know it. We decorate spaces with nativity scenes, sing songs, see nativity images on Christmas cards, and overall have a pretty clear image in our minds of what the scene entails. If you read the text closely, however, there was nothing about the first Christmas that had the makings of a Hallmark card—it was a mess.

A young and unwed couple from a backwater town travel far from home, as mandated by the foreign government occupying their country. The teenage girl goes into labor, delivers the baby in a hole in the ground, with only the assistance of her terrified fiancé, who has no clue how to deliver a baby. There are no available blankets or bassinets, so the new mother wraps her newborn in bands of cloth and places him in a feeding trough lined with hay. The new family is surrounded by livestock, and the first people to visit are not midwives or the child's grandparents, but dirty shepherds who are in need of a long bath. This is not the hospitality a deity deserves. It's a mess.

It may not be the hospitality a deity deserves, yet this is part of the splendor of our unpredictable God; this is how God chooses to enter the world. On several Christmas Eves, I have conveyed the messiness of the original nativity scene in my sermons. On one occasion, preaching in a conversational style, I conveyed the dirt and grit of the first Christmas. Afterward, one young woman called out in a distressed voice, "I want my first-world Jesus back!" What she meant was that imagining the scene in more accurate detail, with all the smells, insects, dirt, blood, and feces, severely corrupted the sanitized nativity scene she had carefully constructed in her mind.

My purpose in that sermon, and here, is not just to relish the disruption of quaint notions of the first Christmas. Rather, I challenge the common narrative with purpose. God understood what being incarnate was going to mean and chose to come anyway. Despite all the messiness this life entails, God still put on flesh and dwelt among us. God came to be among us and stay awhile, because presence matters.

The Word with Us

As we read in the Gospel of John, God came to walk in our shoes. "The Word became flesh and lived among us." There is much to be gained from reading the poetic first chapter of John in conjunction with the Christmas story, but the phrase "lost in translation" exists for a reason. While we can understand parts of the Gospel writer's intent in the English translation, the full intent and multiple meanings of the original Greek are lost in its translated state. This is, in part, because language can be imprecise. I might say "I love ice cream" and "I love my family." Although I am passionate about ice cream, there is a world of difference between how I feel about my family and a bowl of ice cream. But poets and lyricists frequently use the imprecision of language to their advantage; in fact, they frequently play with the fact that certain phrases and words can have multiple meanings. In the musical *Wicked,* the two main characters, Elphaba and Glinda, bid each other farewell with a song called "For Good." The chorus goes, "Who can say if I've been changed for the better / But, because I knew you, I have been changed for good."[6] The lyricist can play with the phrasing because in the English language "changed for good" can have mean two meanings: "transformed permanently" or "altered to become more virtuous."

In the original Greek, the author of John is leaning heavily into the poet's practice of playing with words in the repeated use of *logos,* translated into English as "word." Unfortunately, as with most wordplay, a lot is lost in translation. This is not the fault of the translators, but simply the result of the reality that wordplay rarely translates from one language to another.

Chapter 1 of John is invoking multiple meanings of *logos* in the historical and cultural context of the author's time. John invokes *logos* in the creation story in Genesis; all of creation comes into existence through God's words being spoken. John then leans into the meaning *logos* carried in the realm of Greek philosophy, and finally uses it to point to the ways in which words of wisdom are used throughout the holy texts of Judaism. One theologian sums it up in this fashion: "The Word in John evokes the creative word of Genesis 1, the cosmic and rational word of Greek philosophy, the word of Wisdom and Torah from Hellenistic Judaism, and the person and story of Jesus. . . . Thus, Jesus is Wisdom, Torah, reason, and the ordering force of reality."[7] While English speakers might find the poetry of John 1 beautiful, the depth and breadth of the original author's intention tends to be lost through both translation and cultural context.

Although the Revised Common Lectionary includes this passage on Christmas Day, I think of it as something that is read on Christmas Eve. In services I have attended and led, it has often been used during the passing of the light of Christ at a candlelight service or read when the Christ candle is lit for the first time on Christmas Eve. It makes sense that this passage is frequently used in this way. The beautiful poetry of chapter 1 helps to explain the purpose of all the candles we light at Christmas and even explains the meaning behind the common candlelight Christmas Eve service. We watch as the light of Christ is spread from one believer to the next, filling the darkness with light—a light that remains in the world not just through Christmas but forever.

Who We Are

A few weeks before I finished first grade, a new family moved into a house down the street from ours. The kids in the Kempe family were the same ages and in the same grades as my sister and me, and we became friends immediately. Our mothers also quickly became friends, and within a matter of weeks, we were inseparable. During the day, we could be found playing together, either at the Kempe's or our house, and in the evenings, we played elaborate games outside until the streetlights came on in the lengthening days.

While children from both families had been conditioned to either knock or ring the doorbell, this quickly became an unnecessary formality between our two households. If the front door was unlocked, we let ourselves inside. Our mothers encouraged this practice by the hospitality and love they extended to all of us. While I frequently struggled with homesickness when I spent the night at my friends' houses, I never felt homesick in the Kempe home. How could I feel homesick in my second home? When entering my own house, I usually called out "I'm home!" to announce my entrance. Both my friend Brita and I began to practice this upon entering each other's homes as well.

As children, we weren't paying a lot of attention to what the grown-ups were doing, so we never considered that we hadn't yet met Mr. Kempe, who had been traveling for work in the several weeks his family was settling into their new home. One day, my little sister, who had just turned four years old, went down the street to visit our friends. As usual, she let herself in the open front door. She was convinced they would not have left the front door open if they were away, and so when she could not find people, she began wandering around their house. She saw the basement door ajar and decided to check out the basement.

As she came down the stairs, she saw an unfamiliar man sitting at a desk. Upon hearing her, he turned and looked at her. They both looked stunned, and then asked one another at the same moment, "Who are you?" Dave Kempe responded first, saying, "I live here." He still tells this story, more than thirty years later, and insists to this day that my sister just stared at him skeptically, as if she was thinking, "I know *I* belong here. I'm not so sure about *you*."

Can you imagine what might happen if people felt so at home in our churches that they announced "I'm home" when they walked through the doors? How might that change the way we do church and the ways we live and love? We all long for the sort of places that feel safe, where we can feel at home. But these spaces must also be filled with the people we love. My sister had no interest in the Kempe's apparently empty house—she wasn't walking up and down the street trying to see if other doors were open; she was trying to find the people she loved, because the people are what makes a space into a home.

In 2020, amid the COVID-19 pandemic, my family's traditional Thanksgiving dinner was canceled. For my husband and me, Thanksgiving dinner for two was a big adjustment from our regular get-togethers with more than thirty family members, but we did our best when the day arrived. When dinner was ready, we logged in with family members to have Thanksgiving dinner over Zoom. I am immensely grateful for the technology that allowed us to be "together" during that time, but it was far from normal. Despite all of our incredible technological advances, there is still no substitute for being gathered in the same place.

Two thousand years before the invention of the internet, the God of creation understood this need of humankind. We need to be together. We needed God to come and stay awhile, among us. We needed a God who understood us, in all our messiness and pain and joy and beauty. We needed a God who had been injured and been thirsty and laughed until tears flowed. We needed a God who had felt elated and devastated, who had suffered, sweated, and felt the relief of sleep at the end of a long day. We needed a God who had seen through our eyes.

Sometimes, the moments when everything is perfect, when all the planning and preparation come together, everyone is in their place, sometimes those are lovely moments. But sometimes, the moments we remember, the moments we treasure, are the moments when everything is a little unexpected—everything goes a little awry. Those are the moments when we know that God is with us, right there in the mess.

Whether you have a Christmas worthy of a greeting card or one where everything falls apart, remember that Jesus came to stay awhile because God wanted to be with us. In the end, the best hospitality is that which makes us want to put up our feet, lean back, and stay awhile. As we prepare our hearts, minds, and souls for the coming of Christ in the past, present, and future, hopefully we have made this sort of space in our lives so that Christ is welcomed in and invited to stay.

QUESTIONS FOR REFLECTION AND DISCUSSION

1. Describe a time when you were a guest and felt the desire to stay awhile. What were the circumstances? Why were you comfortable? How long did you stay? What put you at ease in the setting? How did you feel?
2. Have you ever had a home away from home? Where was it? How did you find it? Describe the people and environment in that place. How did you feel when you were there? What made it special?
3. Where have you felt both safe and unconditionally loved? If you haven't had places like that, what might it look like to have that space? Where might you be able to create such a space?
4. Who are the people in your community in need of human connections and safe spaces? How can you help create environments for other people in your community that make them want to stay awhile?
5. How do you respond to the dirt and grime of the first Christmas? Why is there a tendency to edit the messiness out of the

Christmas story? What might it mean for Christmas if we left the messiness in? How might it reshape our understanding of the story, God, and ourselves?

6. How did you experience the importance of presence after the lockdowns of COVID-19? What did you learn about being present from such a long period when most social gatherings became digital?

7. What does it mean for God to be in the mess with us? Why does it matter that God comes incarnate to stay awhile?

Find the companion video for Christmas Eve here at http://tiny.cc /StayAwhileChristmasEve.

DAILY REFLECTIONS

Monday

As a child, I was fond of watching *Sesame Street*. We had several *Sesame Street* movies that had been recorded to VHS from television on our VCR, and I particularly loved watching the Christmas specials. Although the song was first used in 1975, before I was born, "Keep Christmas with You" has been used in many *Sesame Street* Christmas specials throughout the years. There is more than one version available to watch on YouTube. Do a quick search for "Sesame Street Keep Christmas with You" and listen to the song for today's devotional. As you listen, consider how you might invite the spirit of Christmas to stay awhile, long after Christmas has passed.

Tuesday

During childhood, my sister and I marked the coming of Christmas by watching the movie *White Christmas* on repeat while snacking on Topsy's popcorn. (Keeping a metal container full of Topsy's popcorn during the Christmas season is a long-standing tradition for many people in the Kansas City area.) When I combine the thoughts of a desire to stay awhile with Christmas in my mind, I can't help but keep coming back to this cozy image.

Consider a childhood memory in which you wanted to stay awhile. What was special about that time? Why does it stand out in your memory? How can you help create similar moments for those who are still uncomfortable in our faith communities?

Wednesday

During high school, my best friend Courtney spent a lot of time at my house, enough that my mother frequently referred to Courtney as the third daughter in our family. She is a year younger than me, and I graduated from high school and headed off to college a year before she did.

Away from home and my family for the first time, and struggling with some serious health complications, I began to be extremely homesick. I started calling home around dinnertime, hoping to catch my family all together in the same place. On many occasions when I called, I heard Courtney's voice as well. She continued to spend a lot of time at the house and frequently ate dinner with my family, even though I was away at school. A small part of this was Courtney missing me, and being back at our house was familiar. But far more than that, my family and Courtney had come to love one another. Courtney felt at home in our house, so much so that she still wanted to be with my family, even when I was not. Put another way, Courtney had found a place in which she felt comfortable enough to stay awhile.

Have you ever had a home away from home? If so, what were the conditions? Who else was there? What did that space mean to you? If not, where might you imagine having such an experience, and who would be there with you? What does it mean on a spiritual level to have places where we are safe and loved, no matter what? How can this sort of unconditional love from others teach us about God's love?

Thursday

Prior to September 11, 2001, people did not need a ticket to get through security at the airport—anyone who wanted to go through the line and metal detectors could walk up to the gates. While it is still possible to see scenes of reconciliation at airports on the other side of security near the baggage claim, it is nothing like being welcomed by a loved one or greeting party the moment you step off the plane. It often made getting off a plane a lovely experience, even if no one was waiting for you—seeing friends and family members reunite was always a beautiful and heartwarming sight. Even if it was the end of a car ride, have you been on the arriving or welcoming end of such a reunion at the end of a long time away? What was the experience like? What were the circumstances when you saw your friend or loved one? How did you greet one another? What was it like to extend or receive such a welcome?

Friday

One Christmas Eve, after preaching an "embrace the mess" sermon, I received a text message from a church member. She had slipped on the stairs on the way out of church that night. When she fell, she twisted her ankle very badly. Later that evening, she called me from the emergency room, laughing, telling me that she was doing her best to embrace the mess she found herself in. I must admit, her naturally cheerful nature meant that she took my sermon to heart far more than I would have in her place! In the same way, whether you had a Christmas worthy of a greeting card or one where everything fell apart, remember that Jesus came to stay for a while because God wanted to be with us.

Find some quiet time to spend with God today, and listen for God's voice.

Saturday

How are you going to keep Christmas with you, all through the year? How will you continue to welcome Christ as you go forward? How will you continue to build the kin-dom of God in such a way that no one is a stranger to love?

A Prayer after Christmas Day

The invitations have been sent.
The plans have been made.
The food has been prepared and the table set.
The guests have been welcomed at the feast.
We have feasted together and have stayed awhile.
But now it is time to go out into the world
to find those who still long for invitation,
to find those who still long for feasting, for inclusion, for love.
It is time to share this good news we have found.
But we know, when we part,
we will come back together soon.
For in God's kin-dom, there are no strangers.

Christmas Day and Beyond

Don't Be a Stranger

Isaiah 52:7–10; Matthew 2:13–23

How beautiful upon the mountains
    are the feet of the messenger who announces peace,
who brings good news,
    who announces salvation,
    who says to Zion, "Your God reigns."
Listen! Your sentinels lift up their voices,
    together they sing for joy;
for in plain sight they see
    the return of the LORD to Zion.
Break forth together into singing,
    you ruins of Jerusalem;
for the LORD has comforted his people,
    he has redeemed Jerusalem.
The LORD has bared his holy arm
    before the eyes of all the nations;
and all the ends of the earth shall see
    the salvation of our God.

Isaiah 52:7–10

Now after they had left, an angel of the Lord appeared to
Joseph in a dream and said, "Get up, take the child and his
mother, and flee to Egypt, and remain there until I tell you;
for Herod is about to search for the child, to destroy him."
Then Joseph got up, took the child and his mother by night,
and went to Egypt, and remained there until the death of
Herod. This was to fulfill what had been spoken by the Lord
through the prophet, "Out of Egypt I have called my son."

When Herod saw that he had been tricked by the wise men, he was infuriated, and he sent and killed all the children in and around Bethlehem who were two years old or under, according to the time that he had learned from the wise men. Then was fulfilled what had been spoken through the prophet Jeremiah:

"A voice was heard in Ramah,
  wailing and loud lamentation,
Rachel weeping for her children;
  she refused to be consoled, because they are no more."

When Herod died, an angel of the Lord suddenly appeared in a dream to Joseph in Egypt and said, "Get up, take the child and his mother, and go to the land of Israel, for those who were seeking the child's life are dead." Then Joseph got up, took the child and his mother, and went to the land of Israel. But when he heard that Archelaus was ruling over Judea in place of his father Herod, he was afraid to go there. And after being warned in a dream, he went away to the district of Galilee. There he made his home in a town called Nazareth, so that what had been spoken through the prophets might be fulfilled, "He will be called a Nazorean."

Matthew 2:13–23

Y'all come back now, y'hear?
  Paul Henning, "The Ballad of Jed Clampett"

*I*t is easy to love the lovable.

In the Gospel of Matthew, Jesus is asked, "Who is my neighbor?" He goes on to answer this question not with complex theology but with a story many of us know as the parable of the Good Samaritan. Jesus turns to the one who asked the question and asks, "Who was the man's neighbor?" Jesus' parables are sometimes hard to understand, but after hearing this story, it is no stretch to conclude that Jesus' answer to the question "Who is my neighbor?" is as simple as "everyone." In God's kin-dom, there are no strangers.

Christmas is often a time of reunions and gatherings, when we see family and friends whom we have not seen for months, and sometimes years. We spend time with the ones we love, and there is sacred beauty to be found in such gatherings. Yet beyond the familiarity of those we know, our acceptance into the kin-dom demands that we offer that same love to those beyond the circles that include people just like us. We are called to be the light of the world. How will we shine now that Christmas has come and gone?

Cheers

I remember lying on my stomach on the living room floor in front of the television; in these memories, I am four years old and sprawled across avocado-colored carpet with a burnt-orange plaid sofa beside me. Most of these memories consist of watching *Sesame Street,* but I also remember watching *Cheers* with my parents. I don't remember any plotlines from the show, but I remember clearly that every time the show was on, my father and I would play a game together. In the theme song for *Cheers,* we hear the lyrics, "Sometimes you wanna go / where everybody knows your name / and they're always glad you came."[8] During the next commercial break, Dad and I would think up the places I could go where everybody knew my name.

The list we formulated was never very long; a four-year-old is unlikely to have a busy social calendar. Nevertheless, I have vivid memories of playing this game, probably because the places where everyone knew my name coincided closely with the list of places where I felt welcomed and loved. That wasn't the language we used. My dad never said, "Kara, let's list off all the people who love you." But that was how the game made me feel—like I was the luckiest child in the world, as we listed off the places where I knew there were people who loved me (and whom I loved in return). We were listing off the places where I was not a stranger. We were listing off the places where I was known.

Despite social media supposedly making us more connected than ever, a study in December 2021 found that 79 percent of young adults in America reported feeling lonely on a regular basis, and 42 percent of young adults reported always feeling left out.[9] While some might think that this is a phenomenon specific to the COVID-19 pandemic, these numbers are not that different from a similar study in 2018, prior to the pandemic. This information suggests that in modern

American culture, it is becoming increasingly rare for people to have places where "everybody knows your name."

A friend of mine who works with college students once told me that the number one prayer concern he receives is that students at his university feel lonely. However, he has also frequently observed that students on campus transit are consistently focused on their cell phones and do not speak to the other students surrounding them on the crowded buses. People are becoming desperate for places where they feel seen and known. God created humankind to be in relationship with the Divine but also to be in relationship with one another. We need places where we gather together with people who see and love us. We long to be in connection with others.

Once, I was standing in line at an airport in Germany, wearing a sweatshirt emblazoned with a Jayhawk, the mascot for The University of Kansas. A stranger walked by and made eye contact with me, nodded, and said, "Rock chalk!" I smiled and responded enthusiastically, "Rock chalk Jayhawk!" He was clearly in a hurry but called, "Go KU!" as he continued on his way. "Rock chalk Jayhawk! Go KU!" is a chant well known to fans of KU sports.

There is something fundamental within human beings that wants to connect with others. Although he was a stranger and I was on another continent, for a moment, we shared a connection. I didn't have further conversation with him, and I don't know if he was from Kansas, was an alum, or just liked good college basketball. But for a moment, halfway around the world, we were both a little less alone.

When I lived in North Carolina, I used to get unbelievably excited when I saw a vehicle with a Kansas license plate. Although Kansas is among the less populated U.S. states, it still has nearly 3 million residents. Logically, I understood it was highly unlikely that I would know the driver of the vehicle with Kansas plates, but I still had a split second of wanting to follow that car anyway. I was drawn by a desire to feel closer to home, even for a moment. It was the allure of connecting with someone who knows the delights of Kansas City barbecue and would never think to mention Dorothy or Toto. I dreamt of chatting with someone who knows to either take cover or stand watch—depending on personal preference—when the sky turns green, the harbinger of imminent tornadoes. I longed to converse with someone who knew that knitted hats are called stocking caps, while toboggans are definitively sleds. (In North Carolinian dialect, "toboggan" refers to a stocking cap.) The people around me spoke my native language—albeit with a twang—and I was in my home country, but I was more than a thousand miles from home, and I longed for a taste of home; even if just for a moment, I wanted to feel like less of a stranger.

The Second Exodus

The Jewish people in Babylonian exile were constantly reminded that they were strangers living in a strange land, consistently wondering when they would be able to go home. The Isaiah text is once again from Second Isaiah, set during the period when many of the Judean people were in Babylonian exile. It is written as a poem, rather than a prophetic proclamation, but still has the intention of bringing hope to the people in exile.

Chapter 52 recounts the history of God with God's people, and verses 1–6 specifically recount the great deeds of God delivering them from the Egyptians and the Assyrians. This passage incorporates Isaiah's theme of using "second exodus" imagery—the idea that just as God delivered the people from Egypt in the first exodus, God will assuredly deliver them from the Babylonians in the exodus that is to come. Isaiah proclaims that God will return the Jewish community to Zion, a name that is used interchangeably with Jerusalem.

I summarize Isaiah's message in chapter 52 to the Jewish people this way: "You will no longer live among strangers in a strange land. You will be welcomed home with great feasting and celebration. For too long you have lived apart from the ones who love you, the ones who are your shelter. As God delivered you in the past from the oppressive hands of the Egyptians and the Assyrians, so God will deliver you now. You will reclaim what has been stolen from you. You will live in the land promised to your ancestors Abraham and Sarah, a land flowing with milk and honey. You will be home. No longer shall you be used for the amusement of others, but you will be your own once more."

There are times in life when we receive wonderful news and cannot contain our joy. We are overwhelmed by the need to sing or dance in celebration. This is the kind of moment that the prophet is celebrating in this passage. How beautiful is the one who brings good news? Beautiful indeed! Isaiah promises the people that they will soon cease to be strangers in a strange land, an assurance that they are going home. For a people who have lived long in exile, who have lived in anticipation of freedom, there can be no better news.

In the same way that Isaiah uses the exodus from Egypt to illustrate God's promise to deliver the people from Babylonian exile, this week's Gospel reading also leans heavily on the book of Exodus to illustrate its point. The Gospel of Matthew utilizes stories from Exodus to draw distinctive parallels between the origin stories of Moses and Jesus.

Strangers in a Strange Land

If we were to base our Christmas narrative solely on the Gospel of Matthew, our Christmas programs would look very different. There are no shepherds or singing heavenly hosts. The journey Mary and Joseph take to Bethlehem has been edited out, and although the magi make an appearance, there is no evidence to suggest that there were three or that they showed up while Jesus was a newborn. In fact, the Gospel of Matthew would leave us with precious little to compose a children's Christmas program. Instead, Matthew begins with a dry account of genealogy and then jumps straight into Jesus being threatened by the local government in a series of events that look like the characters of Matthew's Gospel performing a reenactment of Exodus 1 and 2. We frequently skip this part in Christmas pageants, as no one wants a deep dive into tyranny or a depiction of the slaughter of infants as the capstone of their children's Christmas program.

This week's passage from Matthew references Herod the Great, who was appointed "king of Judea" by the Romans and ruled from 37 to 4 BCE. Despite his title, there were no illusions that he was a servant of the Jewish people. Although Herod identified as Jewish, he was a native of Idumea. Herod's reign was marked by violence, and he did not hesitate to have his own wife and son murdered when they were suspected of treachery. While Matthew's account is the only surviving record of Herod issuing a command to have the children in Bethlehem killed, the paranoia and resulting violence are consistent with the historical records of Herod's reign.

Herod rules as a tyrant, and tyrants hold power with a great deal of insecurity. Powerful people who oppress others are characteristically paranoid and insecure, which then leads to even greater abuses of power. Herod rules from a place of fear rather than a place of loyalty and love. As such, even the magi's suggestion that there might be another king of the Jews shakes him to his core.

Because Herod feels the tenuous nature of his rule, he perceives a threat despite learning that this proclaimed king is only an infant. In his jealous and frightened state, he issues the most horrid of decrees: all children in Bethlehem under the age of two shall be slaughtered. Matthew draws an unmistakable parallel between Herod and the pharaoh of Exodus 1, who feels his power is threatened by the strength of the Hebrew people and commands that all male Hebrew infants be thrown in the Nile River. We see two dangerous leaders, held up in parallel, whose tyranny is threatened by children. Just as Moses is spared from the violence of the pharaoh in Exodus, Jesus is also spared in Matthew's Gospel. Thus, Matthew is establishing Jesus as a new Moses, an individual who will create a new way for the people of God.

While Moses leads the exodus out of Egypt for his people, Jesus' parents are paradoxically forced to flee *into* Egypt to escape the wrath of Herod. Before he is tasked with the monumental mission of leading his people, Moses is alone in his first flight from Egypt. Moses settles in the land of Midian, where he marries Zipporah. We read in Exodus 2:22 that they name their first son Gershom, a play on the Hebrew word *ger* (meaning "alien"), because Moses says, "I have been an alien residing in a foreign land." Many people may call to mind the King James Version's translation of this verse, "stranger in a strange land." The Holy Family find themselves in the same situation as Moses—out of necessity, they are strangers in a strange land.

In last week's chapter, we looked at some uncomfortable truths from the scriptural depiction of the original nativity scene. In this text, as the Holy Family flees into Egypt, we arrive in even more risky territory that can confront some modern readers with more unnerving truths. The idea that Mary, Joseph, and Jesus all become refugees can be a dangerous one in modern parlance. I once preached on this text and stated that the Holy Family had fled as immigrants into a foreign land—that by definition, they had been refugees. After worship, I was confronted by an enraged parishioner. In the political views of this person, my sermon had done a dangerous thing: I had humanized immigrants. If Jesus himself was once an immigrant, once a refugee, we might have to think of other immigrants as human too.

As social creatures, we desperately need to belong to communities. But our natural psychological need for community has not yet evolved to accommodate the ever-increasing global nature of our modern world. It is easy to be understanding and be altruistic to the persons who are of our own group, but it becomes much more difficult to be concerned with the humanity of people on the outside.

When I encountered a fellow Jayhawk fan in Germany, we made a momentary connection. Like many people, I find long traveling days exhausting, and in my tired state am prone to begin thinking about the people in crowds surrounding me as obstacles in my path, rather than other human beings. Once I formed a connection with my fellow Jayhawk fan, it was more likely that I would see his humanity, rather than simply another obstacle standing in my way from one destination to the next. The list of ways the world tries to turn other groups of people into "them" rather than part of "us" is long and varied, and resisting those ideas can be considered dangerous. What does God call us to be in light of this us-and-them rhetoric?

One of Us

The phrase "don't be a stranger" contains both a re-invitation and a re-welcome. It's a combination of "I hope you come back" and "you're always welcome here." God wanted to be included in the "us" of humankind, enough to experience the challenges that come with being embodied. Being present mattered so much that God put on human flesh and dwelled among us. Surely it matters that we are present with one another; it matters that we make space for others. All human beings are created in the image of God, so something of God is reflected in each of us. Through that logic, there are no strangers among us.

If there are no strangers in God's kin-dom, the circle of people to whom we ought to provide hospitality is expanded to all of God's children. This can create all new meaning when we answer these questions: Who is invited? Who is welcome? For whom do we plan and prepare? Human beings are so accustomed to thinking in terms of groups and labels that the idea that everyone can be "one of us" can be considered a dangerous notion.

Most of us, on some level, feel that offering hospitality to anyone who comes to the table is a frightening notion. Extending God's kindom so that there are no strangers is scary. Obviously, we are not going to begin encouraging our children to accept candy from people they do not know. "Stranger danger" is a real and necessary thing to teach young people in our world. This change we are called to live out in the world is more along the lines of rethinking humankind in terms of "us."

In the wedding liturgy in the *The United Methodist Book of Worship,* the pastor offers a blessing to everyone present at the end of the ceremony. I love these words so much that I have adjusted them to fit a multitude of other contexts when I pray. The blessing commands those present: "Bear witness to the love of God in this world, so that those to whom love is a stranger will find in you generous friends."[10] If there are no strangers in the kin-dom of God, we are called to ask the difficult question, For whom is love a stranger? and then to invite them in, offering them the radical and generous hospitality of God's kin-dom.

Each year, we await and anticipate the coming of Christmas, the coming of Christ in the past, present, and future—but the joy of Christmas is not to be confined to Christmas Day, the twelve days of Christmas, or even one season. We can live out the revelations of the Advent season long past December 25. We can invite Christ in this Christmas, in the hopes that we make room for love to move in and live among us, and not just stay awhile.

QUESTIONS FOR REFLECTION AND DISCUSSION

1. Play the *Cheers* game mentioned in this chapter by listing off the places where everybody knows your name. If it helps, write down the list. How does this list make you feel? What is it like to have places where you are known? What does it feel like to enter spaces where you are known?

2. Have you ever been far from home and connected with a stranger who was also familiar with your home? Describe the experience. What topic brought about your connection? How did it feel to speak of something familiar? What was it like to discuss your home with someone who knew it well?

3. How do you greet good news? How do you greet the person who delivers the good news? What can that response look like? How can sharing in good news bring people together?

4. Why was Herod so afraid of a small child? What was his motivation in massacring the people he was supposed to be serving? What parallels exist between the pharaoh in the Exodus story and King Herod?

5. Why might some people be uncomfortable with the idea of the Holy Family as refugees? If Jesus himself was once a refugee, how might this shape our own understandings and theology around how we believe refugees ought to be treated? How might this shape our understandings of how God would have us act toward those who are "strangers in a strange land"?

6. What have you learned about hospitality throughout this study? What have you learned about yourself?

7. What actions can you take as a group or as an individual to expand the reach of your own hospitality? How might you enact the things you have learned over the past few weeks out in the world?

Find the companion video for Christmas Day at http://tiny.cc/Stay AwhileChristmasDay.

Resources for Worship Leaders

*T*his book can be utilized as an individual or group Bible study, and it can also be used as a churchwide theme for Advent. This section provides liturgy and other resources for worship leaders who are using the themes of *Stay Awhile* in worship during Advent and Christmas. For each week, there are thematic suggestions for worship, including liturgy, worship arts, sermon starters, community questions, prompts for children's time, and repeat-after-me prayers. There are also instructions and a script for an interactive children's program for use on Christmas Eve.

A Note on Community Questions

When my first book, *A Time to Grow: Lenten Lessons from the Garden to the Table,* was published, I was the new pastor at two churches just in time for Lent. Neither church had children attending worship at that time, but I was proud of the prompts for children's time that I had created for the book and decided to use the prompts with the adults of both small congregations. Toward the end of the season, a few children showed up one Sunday. I called the kids to come forward for children's time and afterward went on with my sermon. After worship, many adults were waiting in line to tell me *their* answers to the children's time question. The adults were sending me an important message about how much they valued the opportunity to add their own voices into the act of worship.

After that Sunday, I changed how I preach. If we have kids at church, we have a designated children's time. And just as there is time when the children get to interact, I always make time for the adults to interact as well. I begin my sermon every week with a question related to the topic for the day and encourage people to answer. On rare occasions, I ask a question that hits a home run, and everyone wants to answer. On these days, the response times can become somewhat lengthy. As a result, I quickly condense my sermon in my mind and rejoice because the people are the ones preaching the good news.

Although this practice may not work as well in larger settings, it would still be feasible to have people discuss the question of the day during greeting time or with a person sitting nearby. It can be great to post next Sunday's question to social media on Monday morning to give people who will be in worship on Sunday time to think about the question and give those who worship online time to respond in advance. In these *Stay Awhile* resources, these questions are labeled Community Questions.

A Note on Repeat-after-Me Prayers

Every summer, I volunteer at a church camp for high school students. At gathering times throughout the week, the youth lead one another in singing silly songs. When the song requires the group to repeat after the leader, the leader always begins by saying loudly, "This is a repeat-after-me song!" The group immediately begins repeating after the leader with the enthusiastic response, "This is a repeat-after-me song!"

I have begun using this same technique with my churches. At the end of children's time, we close with a prayer that I always begin with "This is a repeat-after-me prayer!" When we have children who are new to our services, I explain what we are doing before I begin the prayer. If we have a small number of children, I invite the congregation to join in with repeating after me as well. The children (and big children still seated in the pews!) quickly learn to follow up with "This is a repeat-after-me prayer!"

I then proceed to pray in short and repeatable phrases. Praying out loud can be incredibly intimidating for people of all ages, so this gives everyone an opportunity to pray out loud without the pressure of having to come up with their own words. It can be an excellent tool for modeling prayer in our churches.

Worship Arts

The worship arts for this series will depend on your setting. The goal is to have a table that appears to be set and prepared for a feast by Christmas Eve. The best location for the table will depend on the layout of your worship space. Consider where people will be able to see the table settings in your worship space. For some churches, this may mean setting up a table at the back of the sanctuary for people to walk by as they enter the space. For other churches, this might mean putting a table at ground level at the front rather than raised on the chancel. Look around, gauge your space, and pick your location. Remember to check that your setup maintains accessibility in your space.

You will gradually introduce table elements and make them more orderly as the weeks of Advent progress, until the table is beautifully set for Christmas Eve. If your church has Communion on Christmas Eve, Communion elements can also be placed on this table. For the Sunday after Christmas, if your church is small or medium-size, you will need a loaf of bread for each household in your congregation. If your church is very large, you might instead consider having enough bread on the table for visitors and guests to take with them. Keep in mind that bakeries can be extremely busy in the days right before Christmas, so if you plan on purchasing the bread, place your order at the beginning of the season for pickup after December 25.

Items on the finished table might include plates, silverware, drinking glasses, napkins, candles, table decor, tablecloth. There are many ways you might procure the tableware for this display:

- In smaller communities, invite each household to bring an item to place on the table as you set the places for guests. If there are stories behind items that people choose to bring, consider offering a place and time to share these stories with the community. In a larger setting, a few households each week can be invited to bring an item from their own home to add to the table. Remind people in advance that there is always the possibility that something might get broken—something along the lines of "We will be careful, but life happens!"

- If your church has a set of china, borrow table settings from that collection.
- Shop for table settings at a thrift store. Choose brightly mismatched plates and table settings.
- Ask to borrow a few place settings from the local shelter or food bank. Use these in places of honor at the table, and make sure the congregation is aware that the generosity and hospitality of the food bank is being extended to your congregation this Advent season. Consider inviting members to bring canned goods to donate to the food bank as an expression of gratitude and shared community.
- In communities with children, invite the children to decorate plastic plates and cups for the place settings. They could use bright colors from basic paint supplies or decorate clear plastic tableware with glitter and paint pens.

First Sunday of Advent

Scripture: Jeremiah 33:14–16; Luke 21:25–36

Theme: Invite

Worship Arts: On the First Sunday of Advent, if you are using a folding table, you may opt to leave the table folded with a sign that reads "Coming Soon for Advent." If you are not using a folding table, consider setting some folded tablecloths and a stack of plates on the table. A large, visible sign is important for this part of the setup, because you do not want people to mistake this worship element for simple untidiness. If you are decorating your own tableware, this Sunday might be an ideal time to gather people together for decorating.

Sermon Starter: Introduce and explain the theme, "invite." Also introduce the table setup and explain that it will develop throughout the season leading up to Christmas. As you plan your message, ask yourself if everyone in your community understands the meaning of Advent. If not, this is probably an excellent place to begin. Help them to understand that Christmas is not yet here and that this is a season of waiting and anticipating Christ's birth but also for Christ's appearance in our present and in the future. As you move into the theme for the week, "invite," consider a time when you felt left out because you did not receive an invitation. Is this something you are comfortable sharing with your congregation? How does Jeremiah extend an invitation to God's people to remain hopeful while also participating in the sacred work of building God's kin-dom? How does Jesus invite people to be alert with active waiting, and what might that look like in the context of your community? How can individuals participate in the work of kin-dom building in the here and now?

Community Questions: For this week, you might share a few invitations that have changed your own life to help get people thinking. Can you think of an invitation that changed your life? Who offered the invitation, and how did it change your life?

Children's Time: Prior to worship, search online for "free nativity coloring pages." You will find quite a few. Choose some of your favorites and make plenty of copies for the children in your congregation. Gather coloring supplies (colored pencils, markers, crayons, etc.) to pass out during children's time. During worship, ask the children, "What does it mean to be invited?" After giving them time to respond, ask them, "What makes you want to say yes to an invitation?" After they have answered, tell them that the church is working on inviting people to come to worship on Christmas Eve and asking if the kids can help. Begin passing out coloring supplies and coloring sheets. Tell the kids to do their very best coloring, because they are going to turn in their coloring sheets when they are finished, and the sheets will be used to invite people to worship on Christmas Eve. Let them know that there will be coloring sheets out every week through the season of Advent. If it is okay with the pastor and finance chair, encourage the kids to put their artwork in the offering plate each week as part of their offering to God. Use the finished coloring sheets to accompany invitations in your community to the Christmas Eve service(s).

Children's Time Repeat-after-Me Prayer

This is a repeat-after-me prayer:

Dear God,
we give you thanks
that you have invited us
to celebrate the birthday of Jesus.
Give us courage
as we invite other people
to come and join the party.
In Jesus' name we pray.
Amen.

Liturgy

Call to Worship

Our world is filled with fear, foreboding, and desolation.
And yet we are invited to lift up our heads.

Signs appear all around us, whispering to give up on hope.
And yet we are invited to come and see.

Many places, outside and within, have been laid waste.
And yet we are invited, for redemption draws near.

We have wandered far and wide, longing for peace.
And yet we are always invited to come home.

Come, you are invited!
Come, you are invited!
Let us worship God together.

Opening Prayer

God who invites us in,
we know that often we have listened to fear and doubt.

Often we have responded to every call on our lives but your
    voice.
When signs appear in the sun, moon, and stars,
when waves crash and people faint in fear,

when heaven itself shakes the earth,
give us strength to heed your invitation.

Let us turn our eyes upon you,
lift our heads, and stand with strength,
knowing you have invited us all:
we will not be afraid.

Lighting the Advent Candles

Today, we light one candle,
remembering that God has invited us all.
We respond and accept God's invitation
during this holy season of Advent.

As we prepare our hearts and minds
for the coming of Jesus this Christmas,
may we share in God's generosity
and invite all people to share in God's love.

Second Sunday of Advent

Scripture: Jeremiah 29:5–14; Mark 1:1–8

Theme: Plan

Worship Arts: Cover the table with a tablecloth. Set some chairs near the table, but not at their final places. If you are using folding chairs, you might even leave them folded up and leaning against the table. Stack your plates on the table, set out some of your silverware, set out some folded napkins, and add a few glasses/cups/goblets. Do not arrange the items into place settings, so they still appear scattered and not quite ready.

Sermon Starter: Consider sharing a time in your life when—to comedic effect—nothing went according to your plans. Use this as a transition into how, luckily, God plans things better than humans. How does planning factor into our understanding of hospitality? Despite the upheaval of the Judeans' theology and identity, how does Jeremiah call them to plan for the future? How does Mark's account of John the Baptist baptizing Jesus in the Jordan River serve as a sign that God is establishing a new salvific plan for God's people? How can we continue to plan for the coming of God's kin-dom?

Community Question: What event or occasion in your life has required the most planning to accomplish?

Children's Time: Ask the children if they have ever been to a birthday party. What did they do while they were there? What did they eat? What did they see? Remind them that all the elements of a fun party require a lot of planning. Invite them to brainstorm with you all the things they would need if they were planning a party. If they have difficulty, suggest such things as party location, invitations, decorations, snacks, birthday candles, cake, party favors. Remind them that we are in a time of planning for Jesus' birthday at Christmas.

Children's Time Repeat-after-Me Prayer

This is a repeat-after-me prayer:

> Dear God,
> we give you thanks
> for all the opportunities to plan,
> and all the reasons you give us
> to celebrate together.
> We give you thanks,
> as we plan to celebrate
> Jesus' birthday again this year.
> Help us prepare our hearts and minds
> for the coming of Christmas Day.
> Amen.

Liturgy

Call to Worship

> People of God, listen!
> A voice cries out in the wilderness.
> **What does the voice say?**

People of God, look!
The time has come to plan for the coming of God's kin-dom.
When will the kin-dom come?

The kin-dom of God is near at hand,
and the glory of God shall be revealed.
We will plan and prepare for the way of the Lord.

Opening Prayer

Creator God, all too often,
we put too much faith in our own plans.
Help us to trust in the plan you set forth
in the covenant of baptism.

As we continue to plan
for the coming of Christmas Day,
help us trust in the plan of salvation
you created by coming to live among us.

As we consider all the plans we have made
for our upcoming celebrations,
help us to remember to plan for the coming
of your kin-dom.

Lighting the Advent Candles

Today, we light two candles,
remembering that God can always begin anew.
We respond and plan for the coming Christ,
during this holy season of Advent.

As we prepare our hearts and minds
for the coming of Jesus, in the past, present, and future,
may we share in God's generosity
and always plan for more siblings
who might come to feast at the table.

Third Sunday of Advent

Scripture: Isaiah 61:1–4, 8–11; John 1:6–8, 19–28

Theme: Prepare

Worship Arts: Set up chairs in individual places at the table. If you are using place mats, set these out at each chair. Place plates at each seat at the table. Set the napkins and silverware for each place setting in a cluster on top of the plates, but do not lay them out. Line up drinkware in the center or at the edge of the table but not at individual place settings. Put out candleholders, but leave the candles on the table.

Sermon Starter: Hospitality requires preparation—from cleaning and tidying to stocking the refrigerator and preparing food in advance. While people are preparing for all the ways they will celebrate Christmas this year, how are they preparing spiritually? In what ways can the individuals in your community prepare for the coming of Christ? How do both Isaiah and John call for the people to prepare for the way of God? What does it mean to prepare for the coming of Christ and to be participants in the inbreaking of God's reign into this world?

Community Question: What do you spend the most time preparing for in your life? This can extend to the personal or professional aspects of your time.

Children's Time: In preparation for worship, gather the necessary ingredients for making several batches of cookies. Divide your ingredients so that you have (1) some of each ingredient in its own sealed container to show to the children, (2) prepared cookie dough to show to the children, and (3) at least one baked cookie for each child. Stash your prepared cookie dough and baked cookies out of sight at the front of the church before worship. When the children come forward, ask, "What does it mean to prepare?" Bring out the individual ingredients, passing them out to the kids, and ask, "What could we prepare with all these items? Would any of these ingredients be fun to eat on its own?" After they tell you that you could make cookies, respond, "I've got some cookies right over here!" and bring out the cookie dough. Ask, "Are these cookies? What else do I need to do to prepare the cookies?" Let them offer some answers. Tell them that because you are prepared, you already baked some cookies for them, and pass out the cookies. (Be conscious of any food allergies.) Remind them that we are still in the season of preparing for Jesus.

Children's Time Repeat-after-Me Prayer

This is a repeat-after-me prayer:

> God, we give you thanks
> for all the tasty things we can prepare,
> like these delicious cookies.
> Help us as we continue to prepare
> our hearts and our minds
> for the coming of Christmas.
> In Jesus' name we pray.
> Amen.

Liturgy

Call to Worship

> The spirit of God has prepared us
> by baptizing us with the Holy Spirit,
> **so we will continue to bring the gospel.**

> We have been anointed to share the good news,
> **to proclaim liberty to the captives**
> **and release to the prisoners,**
> **and to comfort all who mourn.**

> For God loves justice.
> So we will prepare the way of the Lord.
> **We will witness to the light!**

Opening Prayer

The wreaths have been hung and holly strung.
**Everlasting God, help us remember that this
is a season of waiting, a season of preparation.**

Give us strength to look to you during these days—
not to be consumed by tinsel and paper
**but to remember to stand, lift up our heads,
and remember where our hope comes from.**

Help us continue the journey of Advent
by living into the plan set forth in our baptisms,
**and help us prepare to welcome those
who are still waiting to hear your words.
Amen.**

Lighting the Advent Candles

Today, we light three candles,
remembering that God invites us all.
**We respond and will continue to prepare
our hearts, minds, and souls in this holy season of Advent.**

As we prepare our worship and living spaces
for the coming of Jesus this Christmas,
**may we share in God's generosity
and invite all people to share in God's love.**

Fourth Sunday of Advent

Scripture: Zephaniah 3:14–20; Luke 1:39–55

Theme: Welcome

Worship Arts: Set individual place settings with silverware, drink-ware, and napkins. There are some excellent tutorials online if you decide you want to fold your cloth napkins in a fancy way, such as in the shape of a rose or as a tent on the top of each plate. Place some candles in the candleholders and set them up on the table. If you have additional dishes for your setup, arrange them in the center of the table, as though they are waiting for items to come out of the oven.

Sermon Starter: Consider sharing a time when you have felt particularly welcome. What was the experience like? Who offered the welcome? Why does that instance stand out in your mind? Keep in mind that Zephaniah is not a well-known book in our canon. You might consider offering some extra background to give context to this prophecy. What does it mean for your community that Mary's Magnificat promises an overturn of the world's order? What does it look like to participate in the inbreaking of God's kin-dom? What does it mean to offer welcome to the homesick and weary? How might individuals in your community live out this sort of welcome in the world?

Community Questions: Other than your own home, where do you receive the warmest welcome? What makes it special?

Children's Time: Set up a special welcome as children enter the worship space. Make sure each child receives a high five as they come to worship. Alternatively, prepare a gift to hand to each child as they come through the door. A mug wrapped up with a hot chocolate packet to take home could be an excellent option. Store some pillows and blankets at the front of the church. Invite the children to pull up a pillow and wrap up in a blanket for children's time. Ask, "Did you feel welcome when you got to church today? What made you feel welcome? What makes you feel welcome when you visit a friend or family member's house?" Spend some time discussing how important it is for people to feel welcome in your faith community as well. How might the children welcome their peers who visit your church?

Children's Time Repeat-after-Me Prayer

This is a repeat-after-me prayer:

> God, we give you thanks
> that you love us so much
> and we are always welcome

to be part of your kin-dom.
Help us to welcome others
the way we would want to be welcomed.
Help us be ready this Christmas
to welcome the birth of Jesus.
Amen.

Liturgy

Call to Worship

People of God: rejoice!
We leap for joy at the sound of your greeting!
We rejoice, for God is in our midst.

In the name of God, all people are welcome in this place.
We exult with all our hearts;
we sing aloud and shout with delight.

Our souls will magnify the Divine,
for God has brought down the powerful
and lifted up the lowly.

The Almighty has done great things for us.
God will gather the outcast and change shame into praise.
God will bring us home.

Opening Prayer

Almighty One, you have done great things for us.
Give us patience as we anticipate the coming Christ.

As Mary welcomed the coming of your kin-dom,
may we also welcome your promises.

Give us strength to throw open the doors,
welcoming all your children.

Help us create homes, churches, and communities
where all people feel safe and wanted.

Through learning to welcome the coming of Christ
may we also learn to welcome all your people.

God who invites us in,
may we welcome as we have been welcomed.

Lighting the Advent Candles

Today, we light four candles,
remembering that God has invited us all.
**We respond and accept God's welcome,
in the hopes of welcoming all the world.**

May we welcome all of God's children
as enthusiastically as we welcome Jesus.
**May we share in God's generosity
and invite all people to share in God's love.**

Christmas Eve

Scripture: Isaiah 9:2–7; Luke 2:1–20; John 1:1–14

Theme: Stay Awhile

Worship Arts: Finish off the table with the final items: a butter dish, salt and pepper shakers, serving utensils, bread basket, and so on. Place the Communion elements on the table, preferably in the center, but most importantly where they will be easily accessible to the pastor presiding over Communion.

Sermon Starter: The best part of hospitality isn't inviting, preparing, planning, or welcoming. The best part is toward the end when everyone is full, laughing, and telling stories. Consider sharing some instances in which you had the desire to stay awhile. What does it mean that God enters into the world in less-than-ideal circumstances? What does this say about the significance of presence, and what does this teach us about our relationship with God and one another? How has our Advent journey prepared us for this moment, and where do we go from here?

Community Question: When you are visiting someplace, what puts you at ease and makes you want to stay awhile?

Children's Time: See Christmas Eve Children's Program below.

Liturgy

Call to Worship

We have been waiting for weeks.
We rejoice because the day has arrived!

Because God invited us in,
we have extended those invitations to others.

Because God set forth the plan for our salvation,
we have extended grace to those around us.

Because God prepared us for this moment,
we are prepared to share the good news.

Because God welcomes us,
we have sought to welcome all God's children.

The day has arrived, and now we celebrate!
The day has arrived, and we will stay awhile!

Opening Prayer

God, creator of all things,
we know that Jesus was in the beginning with you.
We have waited in darkness, but now a light shines,
and the darkness will not overcome it.

We will testify to the light,
because we have seen a great light.

A child of many names has been born for us:
Wonderful Counselor, Mighty God, Everlasting Parent.

And now we celebrate the birth of Christ,
ringing in endless peace, justice, and righteousness.

God, your mighty zeal has done these things,
and we will not be afraid.

Lighting the Advent Candles

Today, we light the four candles of Advent,
remembering that God has invited us all.

Today, we also light the Christ candle,
knowing that God came in human form to stay awhile.

Today we celebrate that Jesus comes into this world,
and we rejoice that God wanted to be among us.
May we share in God's generosity,
as we invite all people to share in God's love.

Christmas Day and Beyond

Scripture: Isaiah 52:7–10; Matthew 2:13–23

Theme: Don't Be a Stranger

Worship Arts: Stack the plates on the table, stacking some of the silverware on top. Cluster drinkware together on the table. Clear enough space on the table for all the "leftovers" to be stacked. In small or medium-size congregations, stack wrapped loaves of bread on the table for the congregation to take with them. Encourage them to find a way during the week to share a loaf of bread as a gift to someone they might not yet know very well, such as a neighbor or coworker. In large congregations, stack wrapped loaves of bread on the table and invite visitors to take one home. In both cases, attach notes to each loaf of bread that say, "From your friends at _____ Church!"

If you decorated your own tableware, invite each household to take home one piece of tableware. If tableware was lent to the church by individuals, invite people to take their pieces home after worship.

Sermon Starter: "Don't be a stranger" is a midwestern idiom that translates, "Come again soon." Where are the places you feel known and loved? How have they impacted your life? How does this relate to the innate human need to belong? Consider sharing some of these thoughts as you preach. The Holy Family flees from religious persecution, becoming strangers in a strange land; they become refugees. Consider exploring how we can welcome the stranger in our midst through the lens of the experience of the Holy Family. If the hospitality of Jesus' kin-dom extends far beyond our own front doors, how do we live out the idea that there are no strangers in God's kin-dom?

Community Questions: Where are places you can go where everybody knows your name? How do you feel when you are in those places?

Children's Time: Ask the children, "Where are places you can go where everybody knows your name?" If they have trouble coming up with answers, you might give them some suggestions, such as school, homes of family and friends, church. Ask, "What is it like to be in places where everybody knows your name? How does that make you feel?" Discuss with them what it means to be in places where people know us well. Does it make them feel loved? Share how it makes you feel. Remind them that God knows everybody's name.

Children's Time Repeat-after-Me Prayer

This is a repeat-after-me prayer:

> God, we are so thankful
> for all the places we named
> where everybody knows our names.
> Help us to remember
> that you know everyone's names
> and that we can help other people know you
> by being kind and loving.
> In Jesus' name we pray.
> Amen.

Liturgy

Call to Worship

> We have come to God's house
> because we know we are invited.
> **We are called to invite others to the kin-dom.**

> We have come to God's house
> because God has planned and prepared for us.
> **We are called to plan and prepare as part of the kin-dom.**

> We have come to God's house,
> where we know we are welcome.
> **We are called to welcome all of God's children.**

We stay awhile, to worship the Holy One,
because God longs to be with us.
We are called to worship God!

Opening Prayer

God, to whom there are no strangers,
we continue to celebrate that Jesus has come to live
among us.
We sing praise to you,
for in your love, we are seen and known.

Gifts have been unwrapped and feasts have been eaten.
We have rejoiced in the miracle of your love.
But in the coming weeks, we will put away the
decorations.
We will take down the Christmas lights.

Help us to keep the good news of Christ
in our hearts throughout the year.
Help us create a world in which
there are no strangers to your love.
Amen.

Lighting the Advent Candles

Today, we light all the candles,
remembering that God has invited us all.
We accepted God's invitation
as we plan and prepare through the season of Advent.

We welcomed the coming of Christ into the world
and celebrated together that God walked among us.
But Jesus came only to stay awhile,
and then we were joined by the Holy Spirit.

Through the Spirit, may we remember
that in God's kin-dom, there are no strangers.
May we share in God's generosity
and invite all people to share in God's love.

Benediction

The invitations have been sent.
The plans have been made.

The food has been prepared and the table set.
The guests have been welcomed at the feast.

We have feasted together and have stayed awhile.
But now it is time to go out into the world

to find those who still long for invitation,
to find those who still long for feasting, for inclusion, for love.

It is time to share this good news we have found.
**But we know, when we part,
we will come back together soon.
For in God's kin-dom, there are no strangers.**

Christmas Eve Children's Program

Characters and Assistants

Characters
> Joseph
> Mary
> Donkey
> Cows
> Angels
> Sheep
> Shepherds
> Star
> Magi

Adult/Youth Support
> Narrator
> Cue Card Holders
> Costume Coordinators (before worship)

Cue Cards / Slides
> MOOO!
> WE'RE PREPARING FOR JESUS!
> YOU'RE INVITED!
> BAAA!
> WE PLAN TO GO AND SEE!
> OOOO! AHHH!
> WELCOME, BABY JESUS!

Costumes and Props

Begin gathering costumes and supplies at the beginning of Advent. If there are people with sewing skills in your congregation, ask them to have fun and get creative with the costumes. In case you do not have people who sew, I have provided some incredibly simple costume ideas that have succeeded in the past. When hanging up the costumes for children to choose, make sure the costume elements are pinned or clipped together.

Mary, Joseph, Shepherds, and Magi: Adult-size bathrobes work for all of these characters. These can be purchased new, borrowed from members of the congregation, or purchased from thrift stores. Mary and Joseph will need a baby doll to wrap up in a blanket or just a baby-size bundle to carry. Sticks from outdoors can suffice as crooks for the shepherds. A certain place that sells burgers will give you free cardboard crowns for the magi to wear. Give the magi wrapped presents to carry.

Cows: Use plain white adult-size sweatshirts. Use safety pins to attach black felt spots on the sweatshirts. Wrap headbands in black yarn and attach felt ears. Create a tail out of black yarn and attach it to the back of the sweatshirt with a safety pin.

Sheep: Use plain white adult-size sweatshirts. Add some black gloves or mittens. Wrap headbands in white yarn and attach black felt ears. Create a tail out of white yarn and attach it to the back of the sweatshirt with a safety pin.

Donkey: Use a plain gray adult-size sweatshirt. Attach an oval piece of white felt to the front, using safety pins, to indicate the belly of the donkey. Wrap a headband in gray yarn and attach gray felt ears. Make a tail out of gray yarn and attach it with a safety pin.

Star: Use a yellow adult-size sweatshirt. Cut two star shapes out of a large piece of cardboard, then paint them yellow or decorate them with gold glitter. Punch two holes in each piece of cardboard, and attach short pieces of yarn or string to connect the stars together. Wrap a headband in a strand of small battery-powered lights. Have the child wear the star like an advertising sandwich board.

Angels: Pillowcases can work as gowns, with holes cut out for the head and arms. White bathrobes or adult-size T-shirts can also suffice. Use a piece of Christmas tinsel to cinch the waist. Wrap a headband in white yarn, and then attach a halo adorned with gold or silver tinsel. Wings can also be made out of cardboard and fitted on the children like backpacks.

Instructions

This program doesn't require any rehearsal for the children. The narrator should probably read over the script before it's performed, and the musician(s) or sound technician(s) will need to have the music and copies of the hymns in order and ready to go. Other than a read-through for the narrator and rehearsal for musicians, the most time-consuming part of this program is organizing the costumes.

On the day of the service, have the costumes available for children to choose as they come into the worship space. It is best to have a few responsible youth or adults who can coordinate the kids during this time. Sometimes, to have all the needed characters, it might require encouragement to persuade a child to wear a different costume. One year, I persuaded three girls who wanted to be angels to be magi by saying, "You *could* be angels. You could be an angel, ho-hum. Or, you *could* be a QUEEN." Suddenly there was an argument over who would play the queens.

Adults can easily be incorporated by adding more narrators, musicians, or a choir, or adults can be costumed characters as well. If you have a video screen in your worship space, it can be used rather than cue cards.

This can be turned into a longer program by singing more verses of each song. However, keep in mind that the children might be standing at the front of the church for the length of the program.

Script

NARRATOR: This afternoon/evening, we are going to tell the story of the first Christmas. But we're going to need some help from everyone here to tell the story! So, first we need a little practice for everyone. During the program,

I might ask you all: what do **cows** say? (*Cup a hand around one ear, in a listening motion—encourage the congregation if they are slow to respond.*)

CUE CARD: MOOO!

NARRATOR: (*Sounding skeptical.*) Really? Is that the best you can do? Really give me a good, strong "MOOOOOO!" Let's try again. What do **cows** say?

CUE CARD: MOOO!

NARRATOR: Excellent! Well done! We have cue cards/slides to help prompt you when it's time to join in. Let's try a test run. First, we have **cows**.

CUE CARD: MOOO!

NARRATOR: Next we have the **donkey with Mary and Joseph**.

CUE CARD: WE'RE PREPARING FOR JESUS!

NARRATOR: Excellent! I think we're ready to begin! Our story begins as it is told in the Gospel of Luke. "In those days a decree went out from Emperor Augustus that all the world should be registered. . . . All went to their own towns to be registered. Joseph also went from the town of Nazareth in Galilee to Judea, to the city of David called Bethlehem. . . . He went to be registered with Mary, to whom he was engaged and who was expecting a child. While they were there, the time came for her to deliver her child." As we sing, I'd like to invite Mary and Joseph and the donkey to come forward.

(*While the congregation sings, have youth or adult volunteers help to arrange and organize the children at the front of the church.*)

MUSIC: "Away in a Manger," verse 1

NARRATOR: We continue in the Gospel of Luke: "And she gave birth to her firstborn son and wrapped him in bands of cloth, and laid him in a manger, because there was no place for them in the inn." So now we have the **donkey with Mary and Joseph**.

CUE CARD: WE'RE PREPARING FOR JESUS!

NARRATOR: And now, we're going to need some **cows**.

CUE CARD: MOOO!

NARRATOR: As we sing our next song, could our cows all come forward?

MUSIC: "The Friendly Beasts," verses 1–3

NARRATOR: Luke goes on to write: "In that region there were shepherds living in the fields, keeping watch over their flock by night. Then an angel of the Lord stood before them, and the glory of the Lord shone around them, and they were terrified. But the angel said to them, 'Do not be afraid; for see—I am bringing you good news of great joy for all the people: to you is born this day in the city of David a Savior, who is the Messiah, the Lord. This will be a sign for you: you will find a child wrapped in bands of cloth and lying in a manger.'" Now, I think we're going to need some **angels**!

CUE CARD: YOU'RE INVITED!

NARRATOR: Could the angels come forward as we sing our next song?

MUSIC: "Angels We Have Heard on High," verse 1

NARRATOR: "And suddenly there was with the angel a multitude of the heavenly host, praising God and saying, 'Glory to God in the highest heaven, and on earth peace among those whom he favors!' When the angels had left them and gone into heaven, the shepherds said to one another, 'Let us go now to Bethlehem and see this thing that has taken place, which the Lord has made known to us.'" We already have our **angels**.

CUE CARD: YOU'RE INVITED!

NARRATOR: So now, we are going to need some **sheep**.

CUE CARD: BAAA!

NARRATOR: And to watch over them, we'll definitely need some **shepherds**.

CUE CARD: WE PLAN TO GO AND SEE!

NARRATOR:	Could our sheep and shepherds come forward as we sing our next song?
MUSIC:	"The First Noel," verse 1
NARRATOR:	So now we have our **sheep**.
CUE CARD:	BAAA!
NARRATOR:	And our **shepherds**.
CUE CARD:	WE PLAN TO GO AND SEE!
NARRATOR:	We learn about the magi in the Gospel of Matthew: "After Jesus was born in Bethlehem of Judea, magi from the East came to Jerusalem, asking, 'Where is the child who has been born king of the Jews? For we observed his star at its rising, and have come to pay him homage.'" Now we are going to need a **star**!
CUE CARD:	OOOO! AHHH!
NARRATOR:	Come on, folks! A star deserves more energy and enthusiasm than that! Let's try again. A **star**!
CUE CARD:	OOOO! AHHH!
NARRATOR:	Well done! Can our star come forward while we sing?
MUSIC:	"Away in a Manger," verse 1
NARRATOR:	The magi followed the star. "They set out; and there, ahead of them, went the star that they had seen at its rising, until it stopped over the place where the child was. When they saw that the star had stopped, they were overwhelmed with joy. On entering the house, they saw the child with Mary his mother; and they knelt down and paid him homage. Then, opening their treasure chests, they offered him gifts of gold, frankincense, and myrrh." We already have our **star**.
CUE CARD:	OOOO! AHHH!
NARRATOR:	And now—sometimes they are also called kings—we are going to need some **magi**!
CUE CARD:	WELCOME, BABY JESUS!
NARRATOR:	Could our magi come forward as we sing our next song?

MUSIC:	"O Come, All Ye Faithful," verse 1
NARRATOR:	OK! Let's take a look at our scene. We've got **Mary, Joseph, and the donkey.**
CUE CARD:	WE'RE PREPARING FOR JESUS!
NARRATOR:	Our **cows.**
CUE CARD:	MOOO!
NARRATOR:	We've got our **angels.**
CUE CARD:	YOU'RE INVITED!
NARRATOR:	And some **sheep.**
CUE CARD:	BAAA!
NARRATOR:	And of course, to watch the sheep, we must have our **shepherds.**
CUE CARD:	WE PLAN TO GO AND SEE!
NARRATOR:	Then, we have our glowing **star.**
CUE CARD:	OOOO! AHHH!
NARRATOR:	And finally, we have our **magi!**
CUE CARD:	WELCOME, BABY JESUS!
NARRATOR:	It seems as if we are all set for an amazing Christmas! Don't they make a beautiful scene? Let's stay awhile and sing our next song together.
MUSIC:	"Joy to the World," verses 1–4

Acknowledgments

*T*hank you to my parents, Ken and Wanda Eidson, for all of your support over the years. Thank you to my sister, Kelli Cooper. Kelli, I love that you remind me repeatedly that if I don't know how to do something, then it's time to learn. Thank you to my family members who served as the first editors of this book. I am grateful for how much time and effort you put toward this project. Courtney Strubel gets more than one mention in this book. I'm grateful you are a part of our chosen family.

To my former students Allison and Mike Marcus, Erica Hernly, Kelsey Carnahan, and Elizabeth "E. B." Boresow: thank you for including me in your story. I am grateful for your reflections on your years in campus ministry. I love you all, and I am so proud of the "grown-ups" you have become. Thank you to Elizabeth Hernly; I am grateful to glean from your wisdom beyond your years, every time we meet.

I am grateful to my childhood pastor, Rev. Adam Hamilton. Thank you for the support you have given me across the years in answering my call into ministry, as well as encouraging me to pursue my dream of becoming a published author.

Thank you to my professors from Duke Divinity. To my friends Blair, Jenn, and Sarah—our group chat keeps me connected to our Duke Divinity roots. I am beyond grateful for your love across the years and geographical distances. Also, thank you for letting me be your host during the Great Infestation of 2005.

During my college years, I learned incredible amounts about hospitality from my friend Lynlee Burlison, my boss, Teresa Allen

Frederick, and my pastor, Rev. Paul Smith. All three of you taught me about the importance of creating spaces to call home. Thank you to my friends Casey Newman and Rev. Jill Sander-Chali. Many years ago, when I desperately needed a place to heal (and eventually grow) you helped me find a spiritual home at the Wesley House in Springfield, Missouri.

Several young clergy helped me contemplate some of the theology for this book: the Revs. Mike and Allison Marcus, Maria Penrod, Grace Woods, Lacey Wheeler, Matthew Wilke, Caitlin Bentzinger, Helen Paus, and Beth Graverholt. Thanks for helping me think through some of the cultural implications that my words may carry.

Thank you to the congregations of Crestview United Methodist Church, McLouth United Methodist Church, and Oskaloosa United Methodist Church. Through pastoring all three congregations I have developed many of the ideas and themes used in this book. Thank you to the Institute community for all the ways you continue to teach me about God's love. Thank you to my mentor, Teresa Stewart, for empowering me to continue thinking outside the box.

Thank you to the team at Westminster John Knox Press, especially Jessica Miller Kelley, Natalie Smith, Julie Tonini, Michael Hilliard, and the marketing team. Thank you to copy editor Tina Noll. I am grateful for your guidance, patience, and wisdom.

Finally, thank you to my amazing husband, Mike Lee, for all your support and encouragement. I love you, and I am grateful that together, we keep turning our home into a place where folks want to stay awhile.

Notes

1. Jon Hamilton, "Half Your Brain Stands Guard When Sleeping in a New Place," *All Things Considered*, National Public Radio, April 21, 2016, https://www.npr.org/sections/health-shots/2016/04/21/474691141/half-your-brain-stands-guard-when-sleeping-in-a-new-place.

2. C. Michael Hawn, "History of Hymns: 'O Come, O Come, Emmanuel,'" Discipleship Ministries, The United Methodist Church, May 20, 2013, https://www.umcdiscipleship.org/resources/history-of-hymns-o-come-o-come-emmanuel.

3. Victor H. Matthews, *Social World of the Hebrew Prophets* (Peabody, MA: Hendrickson, 2001), 27.

4. Charles Wesley, "Come, Sinners, to the Gospel Feast," in *The United Methodist Hymnal* (Nashville: United Methodist Publishing House, 1989), 339.

5. "By Water and the Spirit: A United Methodist Understanding of Baptism" (Nashville: General Board of Discipleship of The United Methodist Church, 2008).

6. Stephen Schwartz, "For Good," performance by Kristin Chenoweth and Idina Menzel, *Wicked: 2003 Original Broadway Cast*, Universal Classics Group, 2003.

7. Lewis R. Donelson, "Christmas Day: John 1:1–14," in *Feasting on the Word: Preaching the Common Revised Lectionary, Year B, Volume 1,* ed. David L. Bartlett and Barbara Brown Taylor (Louisville, KY: Westminster John Knox Press, 2008), 143.

8. Gary Portnoy and Judy Hart Angelo, "Theme from *Cheers* (Where Everybody Knows Your Name)," 1982, from *Cheers,*

Charles/Burrows/Charles Productions and Paramount Network Television, 1982–93.

9. "The Loneliness Epidemic Persists: A Post-pandemic Look at the State of Loneliness among U.S. Adults," Cigna Group, accessed November 1, 2022, https://newsroom.cigna.com/loneliness-epidemic-persists-post-pandemic-look.

10. "A Service of Christian Marriage I," in *The United Methodist Book of Worship* (Nashville: United Methodist Publishing House, 1992), 127.

Printed in the USA
CPSIA information can be obtained
at www.ICGtesting.com
JSHW020429191123
52126JS00006B/44